HEARTS TOUCHED
WITH FIRE

HEARTS TOUCHED
WITH FIRE

My 500 Favorite
Inspirational Quotations

Selected and Compiled by
ELIZABETH DOLE

CARROLL & GRAF PUBLISHERS
NEW YORK

HEARTS TOUCHED WITH FIRE
My 500 Favorite
Inspirational Quotations

Carroll & Graf Publishers
An Imprint of Avalon Publishing Group Inc.
245 West 17th Street
New York, NY 10011

AVALON
publishing group incorporated

Copyright © 2004 by Elizabeth Dole

First Carroll & Graf edition 2004

Library of Congress Cataloging-in-Publication Data is available.

ISBN: 0-7867-1428-X

Printed in the United States of America
Interior design by Susan Canavan
Distributed by Publishers Group West

This book is dedicated to the memory of my mother,
Mary Cathey Hanford, who passed away at the age of 102
on January 14, 2004. Her grace, dignity, and complete
and total dedication to her God, her family, and her
community will always touch my heart with fire.

CONTENTS

ACKNOWLEDGMENTS

This book would not have been possible, of course, without the eloquence of so many historical figures, past and present. I thank them for their inspiring words.

I extend my heartfelt thanks, as well, to Kerry Tymchuk, who has served for years as the "keeper of the files." Finally, I am indebted to Mel Berger of William Morris Agency and Will Balliett at Carroll & Graf for both their patience and their guidance.

ON PUBLIC SPEAKING

I STILL REMEMBER THE FIRST CAMPAIGN SPEECH I ever delivered. It was the fall of my freshman year at Duke University, and I was running for class representative. Encouraging my classmates to take a more active interest in campus politics, I did the politically incorrect thing of comparing them to Rip Van Winkle. "Then let us show that we're alive," I declared in somewhat overwrought language, "and strain and strive, that we may say at set of sun, 'So much to do, but something done.'"

Rip Van Winkle woke up long enough to defeat my candidacy.

One of the first lessons I learned at Duke is that the ability to speak clearly and persuasively is essential to achieving your goals. Yet, when pollsters ask Americans to name their greatest fear, speaking in public invariably tops the list. Butterflies in the stomach are a natural occurrence—even for some of the most experienced of public speakers. During my public service career, I have had the privilege of giving literally thousands of speeches. Some were heard by a television audience of millions, some by small gatherings of fifty or seventy-five people. But no matter the size of the audience, I tamed those butterflies by keeping a few simple principles in mind.

The most important of these is preparation. When I began my government service, women in positions of responsibility were still very much the exception. I recall many speeches early in my career where practically the only woman in the room was the one at the podium: me. I knew that if women were to make progress in moving up the ladder, then those of us in the public eye shared a responsibility to do nothing less than our best—and when it comes to public speaking, preparation is an important ingredient in doing your best.

Preparation is proof that you respect your audience. I have always believed that if people are giving up their valuable time to come hear me speak, then I owe them the courtesy of learning something about them. For example, before delivering a college or university commencement address, I learn something about the institution and the graduating class. What are the university's traditions? Are there any shared experiences that have brought the class closer together? Are there any graduates who have overcome tremendous setbacks? I then work to weave relevant material throughout my speech. The final result of my research is that I am more comfortable at the podium, and the audience is more comfortable with me.

A good example of the value of preparation occurred in 1989, when I was serving as Secretary of Labor. President Bush asked me to join a mission to Poland to provide advice to that nation's leaders as they made the transition from communism to democracy.

As I studied the schedule that was being prepared for us, I noticed there were a number of state banquets. Common sense told me that members of the American delegation might be called upon to offer toasts or remarks at these ceremonies. So before departing for Warsaw, I looked up some Polish history and gave thought to what I might say in a toast. And when our hosts asked me to speak at our opening dinner, I shared the story of Casimir

Pulaski, a Polish soldier who left his homeland to assist America in the Revolutionary War. In doing so, he paid the ultimate price, as he was killed in battle. "It is now America's turn," I concluded, "to repay the debt we owe to Casimir Pulaski, and to come to Poland's assistance." Several Polish leaders present showed great emotion during my remarks, and others told me later how much the story of Pulaski had meant to them. The bottom line is that a little preparation made all the difference.

Another principle I have kept in mind is the importance of speaking from the heart. As president of the American Red Cross, I barnstormed the country, asking Americans for three important personal resources: their time, their money, and, yes, their blood, for the Red Cross provides almost half of America's blood supply. In order for individuals to donate these resources, a personal connection had to be made—and I quickly came to see a podium as a barrier to making that connection. I discovered that I felt more comfortable and could make a far better connection with my audience if I left the podium and delivered my message while walking closer to the audience.

The day after taking a leave of absence from the Red

Cross to devote myself full time to Bob's 1996 presidential campaign, I was scheduled to deliver a series of speeches before groups of voters in Iowa. The audiences were surprised when I walked right past the podium and engaged them in a conversation. It was almost a natural reflex to continue with what folks soon began to call "the Dole Stroll," as I was talking about something very personal—the man I loved and whom I knew would make a remarkable president. As the Republican National Convention in San Diego approached, I told the campaign staff and convention planners that it would be much more comfortable for me to deliver my speech from the floor of the convention rather than from the rostrum.

My idea was met with a great deal of opposition from well-meaning individuals. They quickly listed three concerns why no convention speaker in modern political history had ever delivered such a speech. First, they said that even in this high-tech age, there was a danger of cordless microphones shorting out, and my being left in the middle of the convention floor without anyone in the hall or in the television audience able to hear me. Second, the convention floor is always abuzz with activity and delegates milling around—no matter if someone is speaking. Would the delegates remain in their seats and listen to what I was saying? And, finally, some of the women on my staff reminded me that to get to the convention floor, I would have to descend a very steep stairwell in high heels while speaking. One slip and millions would conclude that with the Pacific Ocean just outside the convention hall, I had decided to engage in "crowd surfing."

I appreciated their advice, and set about to change their minds. Sure, the microphone might give out—but what if there was a spare—and a spare to the spare—waiting close by? Yes, the delegates were accustomed to walking and talking while speeches were being made, but convention planners said they would spread the word that my speech was going to be different, and the Secret Service would help with crowd control. As for rolling down the stairs, I concluded that giving the best speech I could on Bob's behalf was worth the risk.

As it turned out, I made it down the stairs just fine, the delegates were very attentive, and while my microphone did indeed go haywire, a replacement was handed to me quickly, and I continued without interruption. The warm response from those in the hall and from the commentators left me with no doubt that the best way to communicate is to speak from the heart.

Making a physical connection with the audience is something that can't occur with every speech, as there are many occasions where protocol (and the fact that the speaker is using a written text for a specific audience and subject matter) require the use of a podium. What does occur in every successful speech, however, is making an emotional connection with the audience. Indeed, this book is the result of something else I have learned from my public speaking experiences—the fact that such a connection can be made through the use of personal stories, vignettes, and inspiring quotations.

For the past dozen or so years, my office has been graced by a photograph of Theodore Roosevelt. Beneath the photograph are TR's words, spoken over a century ago, but which provide a timeless challenge to all those in public service: "We are face to face with our destiny, and we must meet it with a high and resolute courage. For ours is the life of action, of strenuous performance of duty. Let us live in the harness, striving mightily. Let us run the risk of wearing out, rather than rusting out."

I have included that quotation at the conclusion of many speeches, and it never fails to inspire the audience, and to remind me that a particularly compelling quote— inserted at just the right place—can transform a speech, making it more successful and more memorable. I agree wholeheartedly with the great British Prime Minister Benjamin Disraeli, who said, "The wisdom of the wise and the experience of the ages are perpetuated by quotations."

Over the past several decades, I have filed away quotations that struck me as especially compelling or meaningful. When it was suggested that others who wanted to make their speech more memorable or who were simply in need of some uplifting thoughts might find my collection helpful, I was happy to comply.

My husband once described himself as "the most optimistic man in America." Well, I consider myself to be the most optimistic woman in America. I believe in our country. I believe in the innate goodness of the American people. I believe in the values that made this country what it is: courage, perseverance, generosity, faith, and a commitment to service. So it should come as no surprise that many of the quotes I have selected are ones that pay tribute to our country, our people, and our greatest values. Some you may know by heart; others may be new to you. You can rest assured, however, that none have anything to do with Rip Van Winkle!

By the way, the title of this book comes from another of my favorite quotations. On May 30, 1884, Oliver Wendell Holmes, Jr. delivered a Memorial Day speech in Keene, New Hampshire. In his remarks, the future Justice of the U.S. Supreme Court discussed his service in the Civil War, a transforming experience shared by many of his generation. Said Holmes, "Through our great good fortune, in our youth our hearts were touched with fire. It was given to us to learn at the outset that life is a profound and passionate thing."

It is my hope that in the succeeding pages, you will find words that will touch your heart with fire.

Elizabeth Dole

ACTION

A story is told that as Abraham Lincoln was leaving church one Sunday, he was asked what he thought of the minister's sermon. "The minister had a strong voice and a good delivery," said Lincoln. "But he forgot the most important part of a sermon. He forgot to ask us to do something great." The following words provide inspiration for taking action and doing something great.

I begin to think that a calm is not desirable in any situation in life. Man was made for action and for bustle too, I believe.

—*Abigail Adams*

Forget conventionalisms; forget what the world thinks of you stepping out of your place; think your best thoughts, speak your best words, work your best works, looking to your own conscience for approval.

—*Susan B. Anthony*

I suppose when Drake and Raleigh wanted to set out on their venturesome careers, some cautious person said, "Do not do it: It has never been tried before. You stay at home . . . cruising around in home waters. But, on the whole, the world is all the better for the venturesome and courageous.

—*Lady Nancy Astor*

All that is necessary for evil to triumph is for good men to do nothing.

—Edmund Burke

The person who gets the farthest is generally the one who is willing to do and dare. The sure-thing boat never gets far from shore.

—Dale Carnegie

You don't make progress by standing on the sidelines, whimpering and complaining. You make progress by implementing ideas.

—Shirley Chisholm

I like things to happen and if they don't happen, I like to make them happen.

—Winston Churchill

It would be an inconvenient rule if nothing could be done until everything can be done.

—*Winston Churchill*

Behold the turtle. He makes progress only when he sticks his neck out.

—*James Bryant Conant*

There's no such thing as standing still. Unless a fellow moves ahead, he's left behind.

—*Clarence Darrow*

Action may not always bring happiness; but there is no happiness without action.

—*Benjamin Disraeli*

Don't just dream about grandiose acts of doing good.
Every day do small ones, that add up over time to positive
patterns.

—Marian Wright Edelman

Do not go where the path may lead, go instead where
there is no path and leave a trail.

—Ralph Waldo Emerson

You can't build a reputation on what you are going to do.

—Henry Ford

How lovely to think that no one need wait a moment. We
can start now, start slowly, changing the world. How lovely
that everyone, great and small, can make a contribution.

—Anne Frank

Well done is better than well said.

—Benjamin Franklin

Don't be afraid to take big steps. You can't cross a chasm in two small jumps.

—*David Lloyd George*

One hundred percent of the shots you don't take don't go in.

—*Wayne Gretzky*

Never look down to test the ground before taking your next step; only he who keeps his eye fixed on the far horizon will find the right road.

—*Dag Hammarskjold*

I find the great thing in this world is not so much where we stand, as in what direction we are moving. To reach the port of heaven, we must sail sometimes with the wind and sometimes against it—but we must sail, and not drift, nor lie at anchor.

—*Oliver Wendell Holmes, Sr.*

To live fully is to be engaged in the passions of one's time.

—Oliver Wendell Holmes, Jr.

An invasion of armies can be resisted, but not an idea whose time has come.

—Victor Hugo

Life is a great big canvas, and you should throw all the paint on it you can.

—Danny Kaye

One cannot consent to creep when one feels the impulse to soar.

—Helen Keller

There are risks and costs to a program of action. But they are far less than the long-range risks and costs of comfortable inaction.

—John F. Kennedy

The time is always right to do what is right.

—*Martin Luther King, Jr.*

Don't put off for tomorrow what you can do today, because if you enjoy it today you can do it again tomorrow.

—*James Michener*

If you take no risks, you will suffer no defeats. But if you take no risks, you win no victories.

—*Richard Nixon*

The American dream does not come to those who fall asleep.

—*Richard Nixon*

We have problems in our country, and many people are praying and waiting for God to do something. I just wonder if maybe God isn't waiting for us to do something. And while no one is capable of doing everything, everyone is capable of doing something.

—*Ronald Reagan*

Good ideas are not adopted automatically. They must be driven into practice with courageous impatience.

—*Admiral Hyman Rickover*

Even if you're on the right track, you'll get run over if you just sit there.

—*Will Rogers*

Life was meant to be lived, and curiosity must be kept alive. One must never, for whatever reason, turn his back on life.

—*Eleanor Roosevelt*

There are many ways of going forward, but only one way of standing still.

—*Franklin D. Roosevelt*

It is common sense to take a method and try it; if it fails, admit it frankly and try another. But above all, try something.

—*Franklin D. Roosevelt*

We are face to face with our destiny, and we must meet it with a high and resolute courage. For ours is the life of action, of strenuous performance of duty. Let us live in the harness, striving mightily. Let us run the risk of wearing out rather than rusting out.

—*Theodore Roosevelt*

It is not the man who sits by his fireside reading his
evening paper and saying how bad are politics and
politicians, who will ever do anything to save us; it is the
man who goes out into the rough hurly-burly of the
caucus, the primary and the political meeting, and there
faces his fellows on equal terms.

—Theodore Roosevelt

Just do what must be done. This may not be happiness,
but it is greatness.

—George Bernard Shaw

You may be disappointed if you fail, but you are doomed
if you don't try.

—Beverly Sills

If no one ever took risks, Michelangelo would have painted
the Sistine floor.

—Neil Simon

Thunder is good, thunder is impressive; but it is the lightning that does the work.

—Mark Twain

Twenty years from now you will be more disappointed by the things you didn't do than by the ones you did. So throw off the bowlines. Sail away from the safe harbor. Catch the trade winds in your sails. Explore. Dream. Discover.

—Mark Twain

Do all the good you can. By all the means you can. In all the ways you can. In all the places you can. At all the times you can. To all the people you can. As long as you can.

—John Wesley

~ Action

If your ship doesn't come in, swim out to it!

—Jonathan Winters

Do not let what you cannot do interfere with what you can do.

—John Wooden

AGING

At the age of ninety-two, Supreme Court Justice Oliver Wendell Holmes, Jr. was ordered by his doctors to a brief stay in the hospital. President Franklin D. Roosevelt dropped by to visit, and was surprised to find him reading a Greek primer. "What are you doing, Oliver?" asked Roosevelt. "Reading," answered Holmes. "I can see that," said FDR, "but why are you reading a Greek primer?" Holmes answered, "Why, Mr. President, to improve my mind."

It is no secret that over the course of the past century, the longevity of Americans has increased greatly. It should also be no secret that increases in lifespan do not mean decreases in the ability to improve your mind and your community. Although age slowed my mother physically in her final years, she remained mentally active, and was a vital part of the life of her family, her countless friends, and her community of Salisbury, North Carolina until her death at the age of 102.

The older I get, the greater power I seem to have to help the world; I am like a snowball—the further I am rolled, the more I gain.

—*Susan B. Anthony*

A man is not old until regrets take the place of dreams.

—*John Barrymore*

To me, old age is always fifteen years older than I am.

—*Bernard Baruch*

Old age is like climbing a mountain. You climb from ledge to ledge. The higher you get, the more tired and breathless you become—but your views become more extensive.

—*Ingrid Bergman*

You can't help getting older but you don't have to get old.

—*George Burns*

Anyone who stops learning is old, whether at twenty or eighty. Anyone who keeps learning is young. The greatest thing in life is to keep your mind young.

—*Henry Ford*

If wrinkles must be written on our brows, let them not be written upon the heart. The spirit should never grow old.

—*James A. Garfield*

Most people say that as you get old you have to give up things. I think you get old because you do give up things.

—*Theodore Green*

If you rest, you rust.

—*Helen Hayes*

You are never too old to set another goal or to dream a new dream.

—*C. S. Lewis*

There is a fountain of youth. It is your mind, your talents, the creativity you bring to your life and the lives of people you love. When you learn to tap this source, you will truly have defeated age.

—*Sophia Loren*

Nobody grows old by merely living a number of years. People grow old only by deserting their ideals. Years may wrinkle the skin, but to give up interest wrinkles the soul.

—*Douglas MacArthur*

Old age is like a plane flying through a storm. Once you're aboard, there's nothing you can do.

—*Golda Meir*

Age is mind over matter. If you don't mind, it doesn't matter.

—*Leroy "Satchel" Paige*

Live your life and forget your age.

—*Norman Vincent Peale*

Age is nothing but experience, and some of us are more experienced than others.

—*Andy Rooney*

I could not at any age be content to take my place in a corner by the fireside and simply look on. Life was meant to be lived. One must never, for whatever reason, turn one's back on life.

—*Eleanor Roosevelt*

Just remember when you're over the hill, you begin to pick up speed.

—*Charles Schultz*

It's not the years in your life but the life in your years that counts.

—*Adlai Stevenson*

Don't complain about growing old—many people don't have that privilege.

—*Earl Warren*

The longer I live, the more beautiful life becomes.

—*Frank Lloyd Wright*

AMERICA AND AMERICANS

Since I was sworn in as a senator in January 2003, hardly a day has gone by when my office hasn't received a letter or a phone call from a constituent wanting help in bringing a loved one or family member into America. I am still waiting, however, for my first letter or call from someone wanting help in getting out of America. I believe that speaks volumes about our country.

I am well aware of the toil and blood and treasure it will cost to maintain this Declaration, and support and defend these States. Yet through all the gloom I can see the rays of ravishing light and glory. I can see that the end is worth more than the means.

—John Adams

Americans are generous and strong and decent, not because we believe in ourselves, but because we hold beliefs beyond ourselves. When this spirit of citizenship is missing, no government program can replace it. When this spirit is present, no wrong can stand against it.

—George W. Bush

People, when they first come to America, whether as travelers or settlers, become aware of a new and agreeable feeling: that the whole country is their oyster.

—Alistair Cooke

America is about families who want to leave the next generation better off. It's about small towns and communities and neighborhoods in big cities where people look out for each other, and care about each other.

—*Bob Dole*

I found out in later years that we were very poor, but the glory of America is that we didn't know it then. All that we knew was that our parents . . . could say to us: Opportunity is about you. Reach out and take it.

—*Dwight David Eisenhower*

I don't hold with those who say, "America must never change." Our country has always changed. When it ceases to change it will cease to be America.

—*Benjamin Fairless*

I am proud of America, and I am proud to be an American. Life will be a little better here for my children than for me. I believe this not because I am told to believe it, but because life has been better for me than it was for my father and my mother. I know it will be better for my children because my hands, my brains, my voice, and my vote can help make it happen.

—*Gerald Ford*

Ours is the only country deliberately founded on a good idea.

—*John Gunther*

My country owes me nothing. It gave me, as it gives to every boy and girl, a chance. It gave me schooling, independence of action, opportunity for service and honor. In no other land could a boy from a country village, without inheritance or influential friends, look forward with unbounded hope.

—*Herbert Hoover*

What we need are critical lovers of America—patriots
who express their faith in their country by working to
improve it.

—Hubert H. Humphrey

We are the standard-bearers in the only really authentic
revolution, the democratic revolution against tyrannies.
Our strength is not to be measured by our military
capacity alone, by our industry, or by our technology.
We will be remembered, not for the power of our
weapons, but for the power of our compassion, our dedication to human welfare.

—Hubert H. Humphrey

What constitutes an American? Not color nor race nor
religion. Not the pedigree of his family nor the place of his
birth. Not the coincidence of his citizenship. An American
is one who loves justice and believes in the dignity of man.
An American is one who will fight for his freedom and
that of his neighbor. An American is one who will sacrifice
property, ease, and security in order that he and his children may retain the rights of all free men.

—Harold Ickes

This is what America is all about. It is the uncrossed desert and the unclimbed ridge. It is the star that is not reached and the harvest that is sleeping in the unplowed ground.

—*Lyndon B. Johnson*

It's a dream about America, what it means and what it can become, a place where we look to the stars and explore the heavens, but never turn aside from those in need, in the forgotten corners of our country.

—*Edward M. Kennedy*

The American, by nature, is optimistic. He is experimental, an inventor, and a builder who builds best when called upon to build greatly.

—*John F. Kennedy*

All of us, from the wealthiest and most powerful of men, to the weakest and hungriest of children, share one precious possession: the name "American."

—*Robert F. Kennedy*

We must always remember that America is a great nation today not because of what government did for people, but because of what people did for themselves and one another.

—*Richard Nixon*

Our citizenship in the United States is our national character. Our citizenship in any particular state is only our local distinction. By the latter we are known at home, by the former to the world. Our great title is Americans.

—*Thomas Paine*

Never lose faith in America. Its faults are ours to fix, not to curse.

—*Colin Powell*

Our revolution did not end at Yorktown. More than two centuries later, America remains on a voyage of discovery, a land that has never become, but is always in the act of becoming.

—*Ronald Reagan*

This nation has no mission of mediocrity. We were never meant to be second best. The spirit that built our country was bold, not timid. It was a spirit of pride, confidence, and courage that we could do anything.

—*Ronald Reagan*

America is not just a power; it is a promise. It is not enough for our country to be extraordinary in might; it must be exemplary in meaning. Our honor and our role in the world finally depend on the living proof that we are a just society.

—*Nelson Rockefeller*

There are those, I know, who will reply that the liberty of humanity, the freedom of man and mind is nothing but a dream. They are right. It is the American dream.

—*Franklin D. Roosevelt*

This country will not be a really good place for any of us to live in if it is not a really good place for all of us to live in.

—*Theodore Roosevelt*

I see America, not in the setting sun of a black night of despair ahead of us, I see America in the crimson light of a rising sun fresh from the burning, creative hand of God. I see great days ahead, great days possible to men and women of will and vision . . .

—*Carl Sandburg*

Throughout its history, America has given hope, comfort and inspiration to freedom's cause in all lands. The reservoir of good will and respect for America was not built up by American arms or intrigue; it was built upon our deep dedication to the cause of human liberty and welfare.

—*Adlai Stevenson*

America was not built on fear. America was built on courage, on imagination, and on an unbeatable determination to do the job at hand.

—*Harry S. Truman*

The genius of the United States is not best or most in its executives or legislatures nor in its ambassadors or authors, or colleges or churches or parlors, nor even its newspapers or inventors—but always most in the common people, south, north, west, east, in all its states, through all its mighty amplitude.

—Walt Whitman

The business of America is not business. Neither is it war. The business of America is justice and securing the blessings of liberty.

—George Will

America . . . is the only place where miracles not only happen, but where they happen all the time.

—Thomas Wolfe

BUSINESS

When I graduated from Duke University, my brother John, who had taken over the family business begun by my grandfather, offered to tailor a job that would fit my interests. While I chose another direction, I also knew from watching my father and brother that there are few more challenging or meaningful occupations than running a business. I know that jobs are not created in the committee rooms of Capitol Hill—they are created in the dreams of businessmen and women, and in workplaces across America. All too often, government officials neglect to say "thank you" to the men and women who keep our private enterprise system moving forward.

Some see private enterprise as the predatory target to be shot, others as a cow to be milked, but few are those who see it as the sturdy horse pulling the wagon.

—*Winston Churchill*

Business is never so healthy as when, like a chicken, it must do a certain amount of scratching for what it gets.

—*Henry Ford*

Economic freedom is an indispensable means toward the achievement of political freedom.

—*Milton Friedman*

Science and time and necessity have propelled us, the United States, to be the general store for the world. . . . Most of all, merchants, for a better way of life.

—*Lady Bird Johnson*

Business—more than any other occupation—is a
continual dealing with the future; it is a continual
calculation, an instinctive exercise in foresight.

—Henry Luce

Entrepreneurs share a faith in a bright future. They have
a clear vision of where they are going and what they are
doing, and they have a pressing need to succeed. If I
didn't know better, I would be tempted to say that
"entrepreneur" is another word for "American."

—Ronald Reagan

When you're talking about the strength and character of
America, you're talking about the small business community, about the owners of that store down the street,
the faithful who support their churches and defend
their freedom, and all the brave men and women who
are not afraid to take risks and invest in the future to
build a better America.

—Ronald Reagan

Success in business requires training and discipline and hard work. But if you're not frightened by these things, the opportunities are just as great today as they ever were.

—*David Rockefeller*

True individual freedom cannot exist without economic security and independence. People who are hungry and out of a job are the stuff of which dictatorships are made.

—*Franklin D. Roosevelt*

EDUCATION AND TEACHERS

It was once said that a school is a "building with four walls on the outside and tomorrow on the inside." There can be no doubt that America's future is largely dependent on the success of our schools. One of the most enjoyable and challenging times of my life was serving as a student teacher in a suburban Boston high school. Assigned to teach history to a class of eleventh graders, I avoided a dull recitation of names and dates in hopes of bringing history to life. When my class was studying the historic Boston police strike of 1919, I found a surviving member of the striking force, and brought him to class, where he mesmerized my students. Teaching is a high and honorable calling, and those who dedicate their careers to opening the minds of America's future are true heroes.

Real education should educate us out of self into something far finer; into a selflessness which links us with
all humanity.

—Lady Nancy Astor

If you think education is expensive, try ignorance.

—Derek Bok

Education is learning what you didn't even know you
didn't know.

—Daniel Boorstin

Education is the key to unlock the golden door of
freedom.

—George Washington Carver

Education is simply the soul of a society as it passes
from one generation to another.

—G. K. Chesterton

Education is not preparation for life; education is life itself.

—John Dewey

Upon the education of the people of this country the fate of this country depends.

—Benjamin Disraeli

It is the supreme art of the teacher to awaken joy in creative expression and knowledge.

—Albert Einstein

A good teacher has been defined as an individual who can understand those who are not very good at explaining, and explain to those who are not very good at understanding.

—Dwight David Eisenhower

The purpose of an education is to replace an empty mind with an open one.

—*Malcolm Forbes*

Education is the ability to listen to almost anything without losing your temper or your self-confidence.

—*Robert Frost*

Next in importance to freedom and justice is popular education, without which neither freedom nor justice can be permanently maintained.

—*James A. Garfield*

Teachers believe they have a gift for giving; it drives them with the same irrepressible drive that drives others to create a work of art or a market or a building.

—*A. Bartlett Giamatti*

He who opens a school door, closes a prison.

—Victor Hugo

In a completely rational society, the best of us would be teachers and the rest of us would have to settle for something less.

—Lee Iacocca

The classroom—not the trench—is the frontier of freedom now and forevermore.

—Lyndon Johnson

I was only a little mass of possibilities. It was my teacher who unfolded and developed them.

—Helen Keller

A child miseducated is a child lost.

—John F. Kennedy

Intelligence plus character—that is the goal of true education.

—*Martin Luther King, Jr.*

The best of all things is to learn. Money can be lost or stolen, health and strength may fail, but what you have committed to your mind is yours forever.

—*Louis L'Amour*

The education of a man is never completed until he dies.

—*Robert E. Lee*

Education, then, beyond all other devices of human origin, is the great equalizer of the conditions of man— the balance wheel of the social machinery.

—*Horace Mann*

I find television very educating. The minute somebody
turns it on, I go into the library and read a book.

—*Groucho Marx*

I touch the future. I teach.

—*Christa McAuliffe*

The question to be asked at the end of an educational
step is not "What has the student learned?" but "What
has the student become?"

—*James Monroe*

The dream begins, most of the time, with a teacher who
believes in you, who tugs and pushes and leads you on
to the next plateau, sometimes poking you with a sharp
stick called truth.

—*Dan Rather*

[Teaching] is a sacred mission. In the words of Henry
Adams, "A teacher affects eternity" . . . A teacher, as
tiring and routine as [their] daily duties may sometime
seem, is a keeper of the American dream, the American
future. By informing and exercising young minds, by
transmitting learning and values, [they] are the vital link
between all that is most precious in our national her-
itage and our children and grandchildren, who will
some day take up the burdens of guiding the greatest,
freest society on Earth.

—Ronald Reagan

There must be higher yearning equal to or surpassing
the higher learning. A university is a place where ancient
tradition thrives alongside the most revolutionary of
ideas. Perhaps as no other institution, a university is
simultaneously committed to the day before yesterday
and the day after tomorrow.

—Ronald Reagan

The gains of education are never really lost. Books may be burned and cities sacked, but truth, like the yearning for freedom, lives in the hearts of humble men.

—Franklin D. Roosevelt

To educate a man in mind and not in morals is to educate a menace to society.

—Theodore Roosevelt

To me, the sole hope of human salvation lies in teaching.

—George Bernard Shaw

Education is what survives when what has been learned has been forgotten.

—B. F. Skinner

Every home is perforce a good or bad educational center. It does its work in spite of every effort to shrink or supplement it. No teacher can entirely undo what it does, be that good or bad.

—Ida Tarbell

Human history becomes more and more a race between education and catastrophe.

—H. G. Wells

Education is not the filling of a bucket, but the lighting of a fire.

—W. B. Yeats

FAITH

It should come as no surprise that Ronald Reagan is the source of a number of quotes in this book. "The Great Communicator" will always be remembered as one of the most eloquent of America's presidents. As a member of his White House staff and his cabinet, I was privileged to have a ringside seat for many of his most famous speeches. But the words of President Reagan that inspire me most were ones he shared with me when I served as Assistant to the President for Public Liaison. As we sat alone in a "holding room" prior to a speech he was to give to a constituent group, I said, "Mr. President, you have the weight of the world on your shoulders, yet you are always so kind and so gracious. How do you do it?"

He sat back and said, "Well, Elizabeth, when I was governor of California, each morning began with someone standing before my desk describing yet another disaster. The feeling of stress became almost unbearable. I had the urge to look over my shoulder for someone I could pass the problem to. One day I

*realized that I was looking in the wrong direction. I looked up
instead of back. I'm still looking up. I couldn't face one more day
in this office if I didn't know I could ask God's help and it would
be given."*

To one who has faith, no explanation is necessary. To
one without faith, no explanation is possible.

—*St. Thomas Aquinas*

Faith is not simply a patience which passively suffers
until the storm is past. Rather, it is a spirit which bears
things—with resignation, yes, but above all with blazing,
serene hope.

—*Corazon Aquino*

Every tomorrow has two handles. We can take hold of it
with the handle of anxiety or the handle of faith.

—*Henry Ward Beecher*

Faith is the first factor in a life devoted to service. Without it, nothing is possible. With it, nothing is impossible.

—*Mary McLeod Bethune*

The real fire within the builders of America was faith— faith in a Provident God whose hand supported and guided them; faith in themselves as the children of God . . . faith in their country and in its principles that proclaimed man's right to freedom and justice.

—*Dwight David Eisenhower*

The best remedy for those who are frightened, lonely or unhappy is to go outside, somewhere they can be alone, alone with the sky, nature and God. For then and only then can you feel that everything is as it should be and that God wants people to be happy amid nature's beauty and simplicity.

—*Anne Frank*

Have courage for the great sorrows of life and patience for the small ones; and when you have laboriously accomplished your daily task, go to sleep in peace. God is awake.

—*Victor Hugo*

We cannot live without hope. We have to have some purpose in life, some meaning to our existence. We have to aspire to something. Without hope, we begin to die.

—*Pope John Paul II*

Faith is the strength by which a shattered world shall emerge into the light.

—*Helen Keller*

Joy is never in our power, and pleasure is. I doubt whether anyone who has tasted joy would ever, if both were in his power, exchange it for all the pleasure in the world.

—*C. S. Lewis*

Faith is taking the first step even when you don't see the whole staircase.

—*Martin Luther King, Jr.*

To disbelieve is easy; to scoff is simple; to have faith is harder.

—*Louis L'Amour*

I have been driven many times to my knees by the overwhelming conviction that I had nowhere else to go. My own wisdom and that of all about me seemed insufficient for the day.

—*Abraham Lincoln*

The image of George Washington kneeling in prayer in the snow is one of the most famous in American history. He personified a people who knew it was not enough to depend on their own courage and goodness; they must also seek help from God.

—*Ronald Reagan*

He who loses money, loses much; He who loses a friend loses much more; He who loses faith, loses all.

—Eleanor Roosevelt

No greater thing could come to our land today than a revival of the faith—a revival that would sweep through the homes of the nation and stir the hearts of men and women of all faiths to a reassertion of their belief in God and their dedication to His will for themselves and for their world. I doubt if there is any problem—social, political, or economic—that would not melt away before the fires of such spiritual renewal.

—Franklin D. Roosevelt

God does not call us to be successful. He calls us to be faithful.

—Mother Teresa

FAMILIES

My mother would often conclude telephone conversations with family members with the words, "Don't forget the way home." Going home is a natural reaction for the countless millions of Americans who, like me, were raised in a loving family. There is simply no more important role in our society than that of a caring parent.

Children have never been good at listening to their elders, but they have never failed to imitate them.

—*James Baldwin*

A child needs your love most when he deserves it the least.

—*Erma Bombeck*

At the end of your life, you will never regret not having passed one more test, not winning one more verdict or not closing one more deal. You will regret time not spent with a husband, a friend, a child, or a parent. . . . Whatever the era, whatever the times, one thing will never change: Fathers and mothers, if you have children, they must come first. You must read to your children, you must hug your children, you must love your children. Your success as a family, our success as a society, depends not on what happens in the White House, but on what happens in your house.

—*Barbara Bush*

Cherishing children is the mark of a civilized society.

—*Joan Ganz Cooney*

In every conceivable manner, the family is the link to our past, and the bridge to our future.

—*Alex Haley*

One laugh of a child will make the holiest day more sacred still.

—*Robert G. Ingersoll*

Children are likely to live up to what you believe of them.

—*Lady Bird Johnson*

Life affords no greater responsibility, no greater privilege, than the raising of the next generation.

—*C. Everett Koop, M.D.*

A child is a person who is going to carry on what you have started. He is going to sit where you are sitting and when you are gone, attend to those things which you think are important. You may adopt all the policies you please, but how they are carried out depends on him. He will assume control of your cities, your states, your nation. He is going to move in and take your churches, your schools, your university, your corporation. . . . The fate of humanity is in his hands.

—*Abraham Lincoln*

As the family goes, so goes the nation.

—*Margaret Mead*

When I approach a child, he inspires in me two sentiments; tenderness for what he is, and respect for what he may become.

—*Louis Pasteur*

We know that the secret of America's success has been our drive to excel, a spirit born and nurtured by our families. With their dreams and hard work, they've built our nation, made her great, and kept her good. Everything we've accomplished began in those bedrock values parents have sought to impart throughout our history—values of faith in God, honesty, caring for others, personal responsibility, thrift and initiative.

—*Ronald Reagan*

If you want your children to keep their feet on the ground, put some responsibility on their shoulders.

—*Abigail Van Buren*

FARMERS

My husband served on the agriculture committee throughout his years in Congress, and now I am privileged to serve on that committee in the senate. America's farm families do nothing less than feed our country and much of the world. They are truly unsung heroes and heroines in an occupation where every year brings risk and uncertainty.

President Reagan was fond of telling about the time he delivered a speech to a Future Farmers of America convention in Las Vegas, Nevada. Someone remarked to him that it seemed like an odd place to hold such a convention. "Buster," Reagan replied, "Farmers are in a business that makes a Las Vegas crap table look like a guaranteed annual income."

Burn down your cities and leave our farms and your cities will spring up again as if by magic. But destroy our farms and grass will grow in the streets of every city in the country.

—*William Jennings Bryan*

Farming looks mighty easy when your plow is a pencil, and you're a thousand miles from a cornfield.

—*Dwight David Eisenhower*

Show me a farmer and I'll show you a man who feels the sweat of God.

—*Robert Frost*

No occupation is so delightful to me as the culture of the earth.

—*Thomas Jefferson*

The American farmer is the only man in our economy
who buys everything he buys at retail, sells everything he
sells at wholesale, and pays the freight both ways.

—John F. Kennedy

The American farmer, living on his own land, remains
our ideal of self-reliance and spiritual balance—the
source from which the reservoirs of the nation's
strength are constantly renewed.

—Franklin D. Roosevelt

There is as much dignity in tilling a field as in writing
a poem.

—Booker T. Washington

I know of no pursuit in which more real and important services can be rendered to any country than by improving its agriculture.

—*George Washington*

When tillage begins, other arts follow. The farmers, therefore, are the founders of human civilization.

—*Daniel Webster*

FREEDOM AND DEMOCRACY

In the summer of 1989, as a tidal wave of democracy was at long last reaching Eastern Europe, Bob and I traveled to Poland, arriving in Warsaw on the very day that the Polish parliament elected its first non-Communist prime minister. Soon after the vote, we attended a caucus of Solidarity members of the new parliament. It is difficult to describe the emotions we saw and felt in that room. The spirit of freedom and democracy were so palpable, you could almost reach out and touch them. For me, the unforgettable highlight of the visit was walking through the Gdansk shipyards with Lech Walesa, the Solidarity union leader who helped bring about the end of Communist rule in Poland.

During our walk, Walesa told me that his definition of a Communist economic enterprise was "one hundred workers standing around a single shovel." "What Poland needs now," he explained, "is one hundred shovels."

The reason behind the fall of the Iron Curtain has perhaps never been summed up so succinctly and so eloquently. Walesa was describing men and women who, under the Communist system, had no freedom—no role to play in the life of their nation . . . men and women with destinies decided not by individual effort, but by the government. When Poland became a democracy, it became a country where everyone could have a shovel . . . where everyone counted. That's what freedom is all about.

Wherever the standard of freedom has been unfurled, there will be America's heart, her benedictions and her prayers.

—John Quincy Adams

The real democratic idea is, not that every man shall be on a level with every other, but that every one shall have liberty, without hindrance, to be what God made him.

—Henry Ward Beecher

There is a myth that though we love freedom, others don't; that our attachment to freedom is a product of our culture; that freedom, democracy, human rights, the rule of law are American values, or Western values. . . . Ours are not Western values, they are the universal values of the human spirit. And anywhere, anytime ordinary people are given the chance to choose the choice is the same: freedom, not tyranny; democracy, not dictatorship; the rule of law, not the rule of the secret police.

—*Tony Blair*

We know what works: Freedom works. We know what's right: Freedom is right. We know how to secure a more just and prosperous life for man on earth: through free markets, free speech, free elections and the exercise of free will unhampered by the state.

—*George H. W. Bush*

Many forms of government have been tried, and will be tried in this world of sin and woe. No one pretends that democracy is perfect or all-wise. Indeed, it has been said that democracy is the worst form of Government except for all other forms that have been tried from time to time.

—*Winston Churchill*

Freedom is the right to be wrong; not the right to do wrong.

—*John G. Diefenbaker*

Freedom is a gift from God, not government. It is indivisible. To have it for ourselves, we must demand it for others.

—*Bob Dole*

The winning of freedom is not to be compared to the winning of a game—with the victory recorded forever in history. Freedom has its life in the hearts, the actions, the spirits of men and so it must be daily earned and refreshed—else like a flower cut from its lifegiving roots, it will wither and die.

—*Dwight David Eisenhower*

We must be ready to dare all for our country. For history does not long entrust the care of freedom to the weak or the timid.

—*Dwight David Eisenhower*

Democracy is measured not by its leaders doing extraordinary things, but by its citizens doing ordinary things extraordinarily well.

—*John Gardner*

Liberty lies in the hearts of men and women. When it dies there, no constitution, no law, no court can save it.

—*Judge Learned Hand*

It is not enough to merely defend democracy. To defend it may be to lose it; to extend it is to strengthen it. Democracy is not property; it is an idea.

—*Hubert H. Humphrey*

In the long history of the world, only a few generations have been granted the role of defending freedom in its hour of maximum danger. I do not shrink from this responsibility—I welcome it.

—John F. Kennedy

Freedom by itself is not enough. "Freedom is a good horse," said Matthew Arnold, "but a horse to ride some-where." What counts is the use to which men put freedom; what counts is how liberty becomes the means of opportunity and growth and justice.

—Robert F. Kennedy

Democracy is like a raft. It won't sink, but you'll always have your feet wet.

—Russell Long

Democracy is never a thing done. Democracy is always something that a nation must be doing. What is necessary now is one thing and one thing only: That democracy become again democracy in action, not democracy accomplished and piled up in goods and gold.

—*Archibald MacLeish*

Let freedom ring. The sun never set on so glorious a human achievement.

—*Nelson Mandela*

Those who expect to reap the blessings of freedom must undergo the fatigue of supporting it.

—*Thomas Paine*

Freedom is not the sole prerogative of a lucky few, but the inalienable and universal right of all human beings.

—*Ronald Reagan*

The task that has fallen to us as Americans is to move the conscience of the world, to keep alive the hope and dream of freedom. For if we fail or falter, there'll be no place for the world's oppressed to flee to. This is not a role we sought. We preach no manifest destiny. But like the Americans who brought a new nation into the world 200 years ago, history has asked much of us in our time. Much we've already given; much more we must be prepared to give.

—Ronald Reagan

Democracy is not a static thing. It is an everlasting march.

—Franklin D. Roosevelt

It is a good thing to demand liberty for ourselves and for those who agree with us, but it is a better thing and a rarer thing to give liberty to those who do not agree with us.

—Franklin D. Roosevelt

All the ills of democracy can be cured by more democracy.

—Alfred E. Smith

Democracy extends the sphere of individual freedom; socialism restricts it. Democracy attaches all possible value to each man; socialism makes each man a mere agent, a mere number. Democracy and socialism have nothing in common but one word: equality. But notice the difference: while democracy seeks equality in liberty, socialism seeks equality in restraint and servitude.

—Alexis de Tocqueville

It's not the hand that signs the laws that holds the destiny of America. It's the hand that casts the ballot.

—Harry S. Truman

Freedom is still expensive. It still costs money. It still costs blood. It still calls for courage and endurance, not only in soldiers, but in every man and woman who is determined to remain free.

—Harry S. Truman

Everyone wants a voice in human freedom. There's a fire burning inside of all of us.

—*Lech Walesa*

I believe in democracy, because it releases the energy of every human being.

—*Woodrow Wilson*

I would rather belong to a poor nation that was free than a rich nation that had ceased to be in love with liberty.

—*Woodrow Wilson*

FRIENDSHIP

Harry Truman was famous for saying, "If you want a friend in Washington, D.C., get a dog." Bob and I have shared our married life with two miniature Schnauzers—"Leader" and his grandson, "Leader II"—both precious, loving companions. But the fact is that Harry Truman was wrong. As Rick Warren, author of the The Purpose-Driven Life, *states, "Life is meant to be shared." Fortunately, both Bob and I have been blessed with wonderful loyal friends who enrich our lives each and every day.*

There is nothing on this earth more to be prized than true friendship.

—*St. Thomas Aquinas*

Every time we offer friendship to someone we do not know, we strengthen the bond of brotherhood for all humanity.

—*William Bennett*

The person who tries to live alone will not succeed as a human being. His heart withers if it does not answer another heart. His mind shrinks away if he hears only the echoes of his own thoughts and finds no other inspiration.

—*Pearl Buck*

Friendship is a sheltering tree.

—*Samuel Taylor Coleridge*

The only way to have a friend is to be one.

—Ralph Waldo Emerson

The glory of friendship is not the outstretched hand,
nor the kindly smile, nor the joy of companionship; it is
the spiritual inspiration that comes to one when he
discovers that someone else believes in him and is
willing to trust him.

—Ralph Waldo Emerson

Be slow in choosing a friend, slower in changing.

—Benjamin Franklin

The greatest gift of life is friendship.

—Hubert H. Humphrey

. . . Friendship is precious, not only in the shade, but in the sunshine of life, and thanks to a benevolent arrangement, the greater part of life is sunshine.

—*Thomas Jefferson*

My friends have made the story of my life. In a thousand ways they have turned my limitations into beautiful privileges, and enabled me to walk serene and happy in the shadow cast by my deprivation.

—*Helen Keller*

Sometimes our light goes out but is blown into flame by another human being. Each of us owes deepest thanks to those who have rekindled the light.

—*Albert Schweitzer*

A friend is a present you give yourself.

—*Robert Louis Stevenson*

⌒ Friendship

True friendship is a plant of slow growth, and must undergo and withstand the shocks of adversity before it is entitled to the appellation.

—*George Washingon*

Friendship is the only cement that will ever hold the world together.

—*Woodrow Wilson*

Lots of people want to ride with you in the limo, but what you want is someone who will take the bus with you when the limo breaks down.

—*Oprah Winfrey*

HUMILITY

My husband loves to tell the story of an auction that took place not long ago at a gathering of autograph collectors. One of the first items up for bids was a photo of former Presidents Carter, Nixon, and Ford standing together on the White House lawn. It had been personally signed by each of the three ex-presidents, and was auctioned off for several thousand dollars. The very next item up for bids was an autographed photo of Larry, Moe, and Curly—the Three Stooges. The high bid for this photo was twice as great as the high bid for the photo of Nixon, Ford, and Carter. Whenever Bob receives a glowing introduction, he just remembers that in the eyes of the American public, three stooges are twice as valuable as three presidents.

You have a good many little gifts and virtues, but there is no need of parading them, for conceit spoils the finest genius. There is not much danger that real talent or goodness will be overlooked long, and the greatest charm of all powers is modesty.

—Louisa May Alcott

Pride is concerned with who is right. Humility is concerned with what is right.

—Ezra Taft Benson

A man wrapped up in himself makes a very small bundle.

—Benjamin Franklin

I remind myself ever morning: Nothing I say this day will teach me anything. So, if I'm going to learn, I must do it by listening.

—Larry King

~ Humility

Just because your voice reaches halfway around the world doesn't mean you are wiser than when it reached only to the end of the bar.

—*Edward R. Murrow*

It's nice to be important, but it's more important to be nice.

—*Thomas Philip "Tip" O'Neill*

Get someone else to blow your horn and the sound will carry twice as far.

—*Will Rogers*

Nobody stands taller than those willing to stand corrected.

—*William Safire*

Break your mirrors. Yes indeed, shatter the glass. In our society that is so self-absorbed, begin to look less at yourselves and more at each other. Learn more about the face of your neighbor and less about your own.

—Sargent Shriver

Those who travel the high road of humility are not troubled by heavy traffic.

—Alan Simpson

Humility, like darkness, reveals the heavenly lights.

—Henry David Thoreau

INNER RESOURCES:
CHARACTER, COURAGE, PERSEVERANCE, SERVICE AND GENEROSITY

When I served as Secretary of Transportation, my mission was America's material resources: our highways, airports, and railways. As Secretary of Labor, my responsibility was the well-being of America's human resources—our workforce. It was as president of the American Red Cross where I was privileged to see firsthand the remarkable strength of what I called America's "inner resources"—the character and compassion and generosity of the American people who donate to the Red Cross and to countless other worthy causes; the spirit of service that could be found in Red Cross staffers, blood donors, and our army of 1,300,000 Red Cross volunteers; and the courage and perseverance exhibited by victims of disasters. What I learned was that no matter how powerful the destructive forces of Mother Nature, the healing forces of human nature are much stronger. May it always be so.

INNER RESOURCES: CHARACTER

I've learned that people will forget what you said, people will forget what you did, but people will never forget how you made them feel.

—Maya Angelou

I discovered at an early age that most of the differences between average people and great people can be explained in three words—"and then some." The top people did what was expected of them, and then some. They were considerate and thoughtful of others, and then some. They met their obligations and responsibilities fairly and squarely, and then some. They were good friends, and then some. They could be counted on in an emergency, and then some.

—James F. Byrnes

The destiny of man is not measured by material computation. When great forces are on the move in the world, we learn we are spirits—not animals. There is something going on in time and space, and beyond time and space, which, whether we like it or not, spells duty.

—Winston Churchill

What lies behind us and what lies before us are small matter compared to what lies within us.

—*Ralph Waldo Emerson*

A good conscience is a continual Christmas.

—*Benjamin Franklin*

When wealth is lost, nothing is lost; when health is lost, something is lost; when character is lost, all is lost.

—*Billy Graham*

My mother drew a distinction between achievement and success. She said that achievement is the knowledge that you have studied and worked hard and done the best that is in you. Success is being praised by others. That is nice but not as important or satisfying. Always aim for achievement and forget about success.

—*Helen Hayes*

Nothing discloses real character like the use of power. It is easy for the weak to be gentle. Most people can bear adversity. But if you wish to know what a man really is, give him power. That is the supreme test. It is the glory of Lincoln that, having almost absolute power, he never abused it, except upon the side of mercy.

—Robert G. Ingersoll

Whenever you are to do a thing, though it can never be known but to yourself, ask yourself how you would act were all the world looking at you, and act accordingly.

—Thomas Jefferson

Character cannot be developed in ease and quiet. Only through experience of trial and suffering can the soul be strengthened, vision cleared, ambition inspired, and success achieved.

—Helen Keller

94

Cowardice asks the question—is it safe? Expediency asks the question—is it politic? Vanity asks the question—is it popular? But conscience asks the question—is it right? And there comes a time when one must take a position that is neither safe, nor politic, nor popular, but one must take it because it is right.

—Martin Luther King, Jr.

Aspire to decency. Practice civility toward one another. Admire and emulate ethical behavior wherever you find it. Apply a rigid standard of morality to your lives; and if, periodically, you fail—as you surely will—adjust your lives, not the standards.

—Ted Koppel

Life is what we make it. Always has been. Always will be.

—Anna Mary "Grandma" Moses

Character is much easier kept than recovered.

—Thomas Paine

The greatest gifts my parents gave me . . . were their unconditional love and a set of values. Values that they lived and didn't just lecture about. Values that included an understanding of the simple difference between right and wrong, a belief in God, the importance of hard work and education, self-respect, and a belief in America.

—*Colin Powell*

You don't do the right thing because of the consequences. If you're wise, you do it regardless of the consequences.

—*Jeannette Rankin*

There's a tendency to throw aside old values as belonging to an earlier generation. Don't discard those values that have proven, over the period of time, their value. Just believe in those values that made our nation great and keep them: faith, family, hard work, and, above all, freedom.

—*Ronald Reagan*

~ Character

A sense of shame is not a bad moral compass.

—Knute Rockne

I care not what others think of what I do, but I care very much about what I think of what I do. That is character!

—Theodore Roosevelt

A sound body is good; a sound mind is better; but a strong and clean character is better than either.

—Theodore Roosevelt

Ideals are like stars; you will not succeed in touching them with your hands. But like the seafaring man on the desert of waters, you choose them as your guides, and following them you will reach your destiny.

—Carl Schurz

Moral cowardice that keeps us from speaking our minds is as dangerous to this country as irresponsible talk. The right way is not always the popular and easy way. Standing for right when it is unpopular is a true test of moral character.

— *Margaret Chase Smith*

What do we mean by patriotism in the context of our times? I venture to suggest that what we mean is a sense of national responsibility . . . a patriotism which is not a short, frenzied outburst of emotion, but the tranquil and steady dedication of a lifetime.

— *Adlai Stevenson*

The test at the end of life is not what you do. It is how much of yourself, how much love you put into what you do.

— *Mother Teresa*

The best index to a person's character is (a) how he treats people who can't do him any good, and (b) how he treats people who can't fight back.

—*Abigail Van Buren*

I hope I shall always possess firmness and virtue enough to maintain what I consider the most enviable of all titles, the character of an honest man.

—*George Washington*

Be more concerned with your character than your reputation. Your character is what you really are while your reputation is merely what others think you are.

—*John Wooden*

INNER RESOURCES: COURAGE

Courage is rightly esteemed to be the first of human qualities because it is the quality which guarantees all others.

—*Winston Churchill*

Courage is contagious. When a brave man takes a stand, the spines of others are often stiffened.

—*Billy Graham*

The greatest test of courage is to bear defeat without losing heart.

—*Robert G. Ingersoll*

~ Courage

One man with courage makes a majority.

—Andrew Jackson

The stories of past courage can define that ingredient— they can teach, they can offer hope, they can provide inspiration. But they cannot supply courage itself. For this, each man must look into his own soul.

—John F. Kennedy

It is from numberless diverse acts of courage and belief that human history is shaped. Each time a man stands up for an ideal, or acts to improve the lot of others, or strikes out against injustice, he sends a tiny ripple of hope, and crossing each other from a million different centers of energy and daring, those ripples build a current which can sweep down the mightiest walls of oppression and resistance.

—Robert F. Kennedy

History is often cruel, and rarely logical, and yet the wisest of realists are those who recognize that fate can indeed be shaped by human faith and courage.

—Henry Kissinger

Glory is not a conceit. It is not a decoration for valor. Glory belongs to the act of being constant to something greater than yourself, to a cause, to your principles, to the people on whom you rely and who rely on you in return.

—John McCain

You gain strength, courage, and confidence by every experience in which you really stop to look fear in the face. You must do the thing which you think you cannot do.

—Eleanor Roosevelt

Far better it is to dare mighty things, to win glorious triumphs, even though checkered by failure, than to take rank with those poor spirits who neither enjoy much nor suffer much because they live in the gray twilight that knows not victory or defeat.

—*Theodore Roosevelt*

Keep your fears to yourself, but share your courage with others.

—*Robert Louis Stevenson*

Courage is resistance to fear, mastery of fear—not absence of fear.

—*Mark Twain*

Courage is being scared to death and saddling up anyway.

—*John Wayne*

INNER RESOURCES:
PERSEVERANCE

Not everything that is faced can be changed. But nothing can be changed until it is faced.

—James Baldwin

The difference between perseverance and obstinacy is that one comes from a strong will; and the other from a strong won't.

—Henry Ward Beecher

When one door closes another door opens; but we so often look so long and so regretfully upon the closed door, that we do not see the ones which open for us.

—Alexander Graham Bell

Consider the postage stamp; its usefulness consists in the ability to stick to one thing until it gets there.

—Josh Billings

Most of the things worth doing in the world were said
to be impossible before they were done.

—*Louis Brandeis*

If we had no winter, the spring would not be so pleasant.
If did not sometimes taste of adversity, prosperity would
not be so welcome.

—*Charlotte Bronte*

Ah, but a man's reach should exceed his grasp, or what's
a heaven for?

—*Robert Browning*

Most of the important things in the world have been
accomplished by people who have kept on trying when
there seemed to be no hope at all.

—*Dale Carnegie*

Never give in. Never give in. Never, never, never, never—
in nothing, great or small, large or petty. Never give in
except to convictions of honor and good sense.

—*Winston Churchill*

Nothing in the world can take the place of persistence.
Talent will not; nothing is more common than unsuc-
cessful men with talent. Genius will not; unrewarded
genius is almost a proverb. Education will not; the world is
full of educated derelicts. Persistence and determination
alone are omnipotent. The slogan "press on" has solved,
and always will solve, the problems of the human race.

—*Calvin Coolidge*

I think one of life's great milestones is when a person can look back and be almost as thankful for the setbacks as for the victories. Gradually, it dawns on us that success and failure are not polar opposites. They are parts of the same picture—the picture of a full life, where you have your ups and your downs. After all, none of us can ever lose unless we find the courage to try. Losing means that at least you were in the race. It means that when the whistle sounded, life did not find you watching from the sidelines.

—Bob Dole

I have not failed. I've just found 10,000 ways that won't work.

—Thomas Alva Edison

Opportunity is missed by most people because it is dressed in overalls and looks like hard work.

—Thomas Alva Edison

I think and think for months and years. Ninety-nine
times, the conclusion is false. The hundredth time I
am right.

—Albert Einstein

In the middle of difficulty lies opportunity.

—Albert Einstein

What counts is not necessarily the size of the dog in the
fight—it's the size of the fight in the dog.

—General Dwight Eisenhower

Gray skies are just clouds passing over.

—Duke Ellington

Vitality shows in not only the ability to persist but the
ability to start over.

—F. Scott Fitzgerald

A small body of determined spirits fired by an unquenchable faith in their mission can alter the course of history.

—*Mohandas K. Gandhi*

We are all faced with a series of great opportunities— brilliantly disguised as insoluble problems.

—*John Gardner*

When the morning's freshness has been replaced by the weariness of midday, when the leg muscles quiver under the strain, the climb seems endless, and, suddenly, nothing will go quite as you wish—it is then that you must not hesitate.

—*Dag Hammarskjold*

In times like these, it helps to recall that there have always been times like these.

—*Paul Harvey*

Be of good cheer. Do not think of today's failures, but of the success that may come tomorrow. You have set yourselves a difficult task, but you will find success if you persevere; and you will find a joy in overcoming obstacles. Remember, no effort that we make to attain something beautiful is lost.

—Helen Keller

If there's nobody in your way, it's because you're not going anywhere.

—Robert F. Kennedy

You ought to believe in something in life and believe that thing so fervently that you will stand up for it till the end of your days.

—Martin Luther King, Jr.

It takes as much courage to have tried and failed as it does to have tried and succeeded.

—Anne Morrow Lindbergh

There are no hopeless situations; there are only people who have grown hopeless about them.

—*Clare Boothe Luce*

A man is not finished when he is defeated. He is finished when he quits.

—*Richard Nixon*

Greatness comes not when things go always good for you, but the greatness comes and you are really tested when you take some knocks, some disappointments, when sadness comes. Because only if you have been in the deepest valley can you ever know how magnificent it is to be on the highest mountain.

—*Richard Nixon*

My feet are tired but my soul is at rest.

—*Rosa Parks*

The secret is this: strength lies solely in tenacity.

—Louis Pasteur

The way I see it, if you want the rainbow, you gotta put up with the rain.

—Dolly Parton

In case of doubt, push on just a little further and then keep on pushing.

—George S. Patton, Jr.

Become a "possibilitarian." No matter how dark things seem to be or actually are, raise your sights and see possibilities—always see them, for they're always there.

—Norman Vincent Peale

Problems are to the mind what exercise is to the muscles; they toughen and make strong.

—Norman Vincent Peale

I do not care how dark the night; I believe in the coming of the morning.

—*Dr. Joseph Charles Price*

Now, what should happen when you make a mistake is this: You take your knocks, you learn your lessons and then you move on.

—*Ronald Reagan*

There are no shortcuts to any place worth going.

—*Beverly Sills*

When people keep telling you that you can't do a thing, you kind of like to try it.

—*Margaret Chase Smith*

When you get into a tight place and everything goes against you, till it seems as though you could not hold on a minute longer, never give up then, for that is just the place and time that the tide will turn.

—*Harriet Beecher Stowe*

To keep a lamp burning we have to keep putting oil in it.

—*Mother Teresa*

If you want a place in the sun, you've got to put up with a few blisters.

—*Abigail Van Buren*

I have learned that success is to be measured not so much by the position that one has reached in life as by the obstacles which he has overcome while trying to succeed.

—*Booker T. Washington*

Nothing is worthwhile that is not hard. You do not improve your muscle by doing the easy thing; you improve it by doing the hard thing, and you get your zest by doing a thing that is difficult, not a thing that is easy.

—*Woodrow Wilson*

Don't let what you cannot do interfere with what you can do.

—*John Wooden*

You do what you can for as long as you can, and when you finally can't, you do the next best thing. You back up, but you don't give up.

—*Chuck Yeager*

INNER RESOURCES:
SERVICE AND GENEROSITY

Those who bring sunshine into the lives of others
cannot keep it from themselves.

—*James M. Barrie*

I had a dream where all America's volunteers were on a
ship sailing for another country. This is what I saw: The
hospital was quiet. The home for the aged was like a
tomb. All social agencies closed their doors unable to
implement scouting, recreation, services for the
retarded, the crippled, the lonely, the abandoned, or
disaster victims. Health agencies all had signs on their
doors, "Cures for cancer and other diseases have been
cancelled." Schools were graveyards. Churches were
empty. I fought just to get a glimpse of the ship of
volunteers, as it would be my last glimpse of civilization
as we were meant to be.

—*Erma Bombeck*

Together, we can show that what matters in the end are not possessions. What matters is engaging in the high moral principle of serving one another. That's the story of America that we can write through voluntary service. . . . We all have something to give. So if you know how to read, find someone who can't. If you've got a hammer, find a nail. If you're not hungry, not lonely, not in trouble—seek out someone who is.

—George H. W. Bush

From now on, any definition of a successful life must include service to others.

—George H. W. Bush

Use power to help people. For we are given power not to advance our own purpose nor to make a great show in the world, nor a name. There is but one just use of power and it is to serve people.

—George W. Bush

It is not the style of clothes one wears; neither the kind of automobile one drives; nor the amount of money one has in the bank that counts. These mean nothing. It is simply service that means success.

—*George Washington Carver*

A pat on the back, though only a few vertebrae removed from a kick in the pants, is miles ahead in results.

—*Bennett Cerf*

We make a living by what we get. We make a life by what we give.

—*Winston Churchill*

No person was ever honored for what he received. Honor has been the reward for what he gave.

—*Calvin Coolidge*

Anywhere I see suffering, that is where I want to be,
doing what I can.

—*Princess Diana*

No one is useless in his world who lightens the burden
of it for anyone else.

—*Charles Dickens*

The greatest good you can do for another is not just to
share your riches, but to reveal to him his own.

—*Benjamin Disraeli*

"The unity that binds us all together, that makes this
earth a family, and all men brothers and the sons of
God, is love. That love can take many forms. It is the
love of one human being for another, a love which
cements our attachments to a place of memory, the love
of work and the sense of mission which must of necessity
replace purely individual ambition if that work is to be
truly fulfilling."

—*Thomas Wolfe*

Service is the rent each of us pays for living, the very purpose of life and not something you do in your spare time or after you have reached your personal goals.

—*Marian Wright Edelman*

It is high time the ideal of success should be replaced with the ideal of service.

—*Albert Einstein*

Only a life lived for others is a life worthwhile.

—*Albert Einstein*

The true slogan of a true democracy is not "Let the government do it" but rather, "Let's do it ourselves." . . . This is the spirit of a people dedicated to helping themselves—and one another.

—*Dwight David Eisenhower*

What do we live for if it is not to make life less difficult for others?

—*George Eliot*

You cannot do a kindness too soon, for you never know how soon it will be too late.

—*Ralph Waldo Emerson*

We can't do everything for everyone everywhere, but we can do something for someone somewhere.

—*Richard L. Evans*

Always demanding the best of oneself, living with honor, devoting one's talents and gifts to the benefit of others— these are the measures of success that endure when material things have passed away.

—*Gerald Ford*

Some people strengthen the society just by being the kind of people they are.

—*John W. Gardner*

A life spent centering only on itself will in the end occupy a very, very small universe.

—*John Glenn*

God has given us two hands—one to receive with and the other to give with. We are not cisterns made for hoarding. We are channels made for sharing.

—*Billy Graham*

If you haven't any charity in your heart, you have the worst kind of heart trouble.

—*Bob Hope*

The impersonal hand of government can never replace the helping hand of a neighbor.

—*Hubert H. Humphrey*

A kind heart is a fountain of gladness, making everything in its vicinity freshen into smiles.

—*Washington Irving*

The greatest use of a life is to spend it on something that outlasts it.

—*William James*

Life is a talent entrusted to us so that we can transform it and increase it, making it a gift to others. No man is an iceberg drifting on the ocean of history. Each one of us belongs to a great family, in which he has his own place and his own role to play.

—*Pope John Paul II*

Justice will never be fully attained unless people see in the poor person, who is asking for help in order to survive, not an annoyance or a burden, but an opportunity for showing kindness and a chance for greater enrichment.

—Pope John Paul II

The path of human solidarity is the path of service; and true service means selfless love, open to the needs of all, without distinction of persons, with the explicit purpose of reinforcing each person's sense of God-given dignity.

—Pope John Paul II

Life can be an exciting business—and most exciting when it is lived for others.

—Helen Keller

Everybody can be great. Because anybody can serve. You don't have to have a college degree to serve. You don't have to make your subject and verb agree to serve. You don't have to know about Plato and Aristotle to serve. You don't have to know Einstein's theory of relativity to serve. You don't have to know the second theory of thermodynamics in physics to serve. You only need a heart full of grace. A soul generated by love.

—Martin Luther King, Jr.

Those who are not looking for happiness are the most likely to find it, because those who are searching forget that the surest way to be happy is to seek happiness for others.

—Martin Luther King, Jr.

It really boils down to this: that all life is interrelated. We are all caught in an inescapable network of mutuality, tied into a single garment of destiny. Whatever affects one directly, affects all indirectly.

—Martin Luther King, Jr.

To ease another's heartache is to forget one's own.

—*Abraham Lincoln*

To give without any reward, or any notice, has a special quality of its own.

—*Anne Morrow Lindbergh*

To see the earth as we now see it, small and blue and beautiful in that eternal silence where it floats, is to see ourselves as riders on the earth together, brothers on that bright loveliness in the unending night—brothers who see now they are truly brothers.

—*Archibald MacLeish*

None of us has gotten where we are solely by pulling ourselves up from our own bootstraps. We got here because somebody bent down and helped us.

—*Thurgood Marshall*

Heroes are not giant statues framed against a red sky.
They are people who say, "This is my community and
it's my responsibility to make it better."

—*Tom McCall*

Never doubt that a small group of thoughtful committed
citizens can change the world. Indeed, it is the only thing
that ever has.

—*Margaret Mead*

I believe that we are here on planet earth to live, grow up
and do what we can to make the world a better place for
all people to enjoy freedom.

—*Rosa Parks*

I expect to pass through this life but once. If, therefore,
there be any kindess I can show, or any good thing I can
do to any fellow being, let me do it now, and not deter
or neglect it, as I shall not pass this way again.

—*William Penn*

I'm not one who feels that you have to be brave to be a star, but that your life can be satisfying and happy if you work to make a difference. The point is to make a difference by the way you live your life.

—*Esther Peterson*

To be alive and to be human is to struggle for what is right and against what is not.

—*Ronald Reagan*

No matter how big and powerful government gets and the many services it provides, it can never take the place of volunteers.

—*Ronald Reagan*

A life isn't significant except for its impact on other lives.

—*Jackie Robinson*

Giving is the secret of a healthy life. Not necessarily money, but whatever a person has of encouragement, sympathy and understanding.

—John D. Rockefeller, Sr.

At the center of the universe is a loving heart that continues to beat and that wants the best for every person. Anything that we can do to help foster the intellect and spirit and emotional growth of our fellow human beings, that is our job. Those of us who have this particular vision must continue against the odds. Life is for service.

—Fred Rogers

Human kindness has never weakened the stamina or softened the fiber of a free people. A nation does not have to be cruel to be tough.

—Franklin D. Roosevelt

The test of our progress is not whether we add more to the abundance of those who have much; it is whether we provide enough to those who have too little.

—*Franklin D. Roosevelt*

During my long life, I have learned one lesson: that the most important thing is to realize why one is alive. I think it is not only to build bridges or tall buildings or make money, but to do something truly important, to do something for humanity. To bring joy, hope, to make life richer for the spirit because you have been alive—that is the most important thing.

—*Arthur Rubinstein*

As much as we need a prosperous economy, we also need a prosperity of kindness and decency.

—*Caroline Kennedy Schlossberg*

Constant kindness can accomplish much. As the sun makes ice melt, kindness causes misunderstanding, mistrust and hostility to evaporate.

—*Albert Schweitzer*

I don't know what your destiny will be, but one thing I do know: the only ones among you who will be really happy are those who have sought and found how to serve.

—*Albert Schweitzer*

It's not what you get out of life that counts; it's what you give and what is given to you from the heart.

—*Sargent Shriver*

Don't judge each day by the harvest you reap, but by the seeds you plant.

—*Robert Louis Stevenson*

Be kind and merciful. Let no one ever come to you without coming away better and happier. Be the living expression of God's kindness: kindness in your face, kindness in your eyes, kindness in your smile, kindness in your warm greeting.

—*Mother Teresa*

At the end of life we will not be judged by how many diplomas we have received, how much money we have made, how many great things we have done. We will be judged by "I was hungry, and you gave me something to eat. I was naked and you clothed me. I was homeless, and you took me in." Hungry not only for bread—but hungry for love. Naked not only for clothing—but naked of human dignity and respect. Homeless not only for want of a home of bricks—but homeless because of rejection.

—*Mother Teresa*

There is little hope for democracy if the hearts of men and women can not be touched by something greater than themselves.

—*Margaret Thatcher*

All of us are born for a reason, but all of us don't discover why. Success in life has nothing to do with what you gain in life or accomplish for yourself. It's what you do for others.

—*Danny Thomas*

Do your little bit of good where you are; it's those little bits of good put together that overwhelm the world.

—*Archbishop Desmond Tutu*

Kindness is the language which the deaf can hear and the blind can see.

—*Mark Twain*

There are two ways of spreading light: to be the candle or the mirror that reflects it.

—*Edith Wharton*

Those who are happiest are those who do the most
for others.

—*Booker T. Washington*

There is no cause half so sacred as the cause of people.
There is no idea so uplifting as the idea of the service
of humanity.

—*Woodrow Wilson*

You are not merely here to make a living. You are here in
order to enable the world to live more amply, with greater
vision, with a finer spirit of hope and achievement. You
are here to enrich the world, and you impoverish yourself
if you forget the errand.

—*Woodrow Wilson*

LAUGHTER

*Life with Bob Dole means each day is filled with laughter.
Bob richly deserves his reputation as one of the quickest wits
in Washington, D.C. I should know, because I've been on the
receiving end of some of his barbs. When he introduced me before
the Senate Commerce Committee considering my nomination to
serve as Secretary of Transportation, Bob paraphrased Nathan
Hale, saying "I regret that I have but one wife to give for my
country's infrastructure." He also suggested the Federal Highway
Administration might consider using my biscuit recipe to fill pot-
holes. I achieved some revenge when I fired back that I knew all
about airbags because I had been driving around with one for
years!*

When humor goes, there goes civilization.

—Erma Bombeck

Laughter is the shortest distance between two people.

—Victor Borge

The person who can bring the spirit of laughter into a room is indeed blessed.

—Bennett Cerf

The most wasted of all days is one without laughter.

—e.e. cummings

Good leaders not only need strong backbones, they need strong funny bones.

—Bob Dole

～ Laughter

A sense of humor is part of the art of leadership, of getting along with people, of getting things done.

—Dwight D. Eisenhower

Laughter is the sun that drives winter from the human face.

—Victor Hugo

There are three things that are real—God, human folly and laughter. The first two are beyond comprehension. So, we must do what we can with the third.

—John F. Kennedy

Laughter is the joyous, beautiful, universal evergreen of life.

—Abraham Lincoln

Laughter is God's hand on a troubled world.

—Minnie Pearl

If I were given the opportunity to present a gift to the next generation, it would be the ability for each individual to learn to laugh at himself.

—*Charles Schultz*

If I can keep laughing everything will be fine.

—*Beverly Sills*

Life is a mirror. If you frown at it, it frowns back; if you smile, it returns the greeting.

—*William Makepeace Thackeray*

The human race has one really effective weapon, and that is laughter.

—*Mark Twain*

Laughter is the brush that sweeps away the cobwebs of your heart.

—*Mort Walker*

LEADERSHIP

I have seen many definitions and examples of outstanding leadership during my years in public service, but perhaps the best are words that the author hoped would never be read or heard. They are the words of Dwight Eisenhower, written the night before the D-day invasion—to be released to the press and the world if the invasion was a failure.

"Our landings have failed," he wrote. "And I have withdrawn the troops. My decision to attack at this time and place was based upon the best information available. The troops, the air, and the navy did all that bravery and devotion could do. If any blame or fault attaches to the attempt, it is mine, and mine alone."

"If any blame or fault attaches to the attempt, it is mine, and mine alone." There, in one simple sentence, is true leadership. How many of our societal problems would vanish overnight if we could just get those words right: The responsibility is mine alone.

In the final analysis, that is what great leaders do—not just in Washington, D.C., but in cities and communities all across America. They don't pass the responsibility or blame to someone else. They stand ready to make the hard decisions, and to live with failure or success. America is for the better because we have been blessed with leaders willing to do just that.

I see it said that leaders should keep their ears to the ground. All I can say is that the British nation will find it very hard to look up to leaders who are detected in that somewhat ungainly posture.

—*Winston Churchill*

I would rather try to persuade a man to go along, because once I have persuaded him he will stick. If I scare him, he will stay just as long as he is scared, and then he is gone.

—*Dwight David Eisenhower*

All of the great leaders have had one characteristic in common: it was the willingness to confront unequivocally the major anxiety of their people in their time. This, and not much else, is the essence of leadership.

—*John Kenneth Galbraith*

Leaders can express the values that hold the society together. Most important, they can conceive and articulate goals that lift people out of their petty preoccupations, carry them above the conflicts that tear a society apart, and unite them in the pursuit of objectives worthy of their best efforts.

—*John W. Gardner*

This is what leadership is all about: staking your ground ahead of where opinion is and convincing people, not simply following the popular opinion of the moment.

—*Doris Kearns Goodwin*

The very essence of leadership is that you have to have a vision. It's got to be a vision you articulate clearly and forcefully on every occasion. You can't blow an uncertain trumpet.

—*Father Theodore Hesburgh*

To be a leader means willingness to risk—and a willingness to love. Has the leader given you something from the heart?

—*Hubert H. Humphrey*

A good leader is not a searcher of consensus, but a molder of consensus..

—*Martin Luther King, Jr.*

The task of a leader is to get his people from where they are to where they have not been.

—*Henry Kissinger*

The truth is that many people set rules to keep from making decisions. Not me. I don't want to be a manager or a dictator. I want to be a leader—and leadership is ongoing, adjustable, flexible, and dynamic.

—*Mike Krzyzewski*

Nearly all men can stand adversity, but if you want to test a man's character, give him power.

—*Abraham Lincoln*

The final test of a leader is that he leaves behind in other men the conviction and the will to carry on.

—*Walter Lippman*

Leadership is the capacity and will to rally men and women to a common purpose and the character which inspires confidence.

—*Bernard Montgomery*

Never tell people how to do things. Tell them what to do and they will surprise you with their ingenuity.

—*General George S. Patton, Jr.*

Great leaders are almost always great simplifiers, who can cut through argument, debate, and doubt to offer a solution everyone can understand.

—*Colin Powell*

You cannot be a leader and ask other people to follow you, unless you know how to follow, too.

—*Sam Rayburn*

A leader, once convinced a particular course of action is the right one, must have the determination to stick with it and be undaunted when the going gets tough.

—*Ronald Reagan*

～ Leadership

A great leader is not necessarily one who does the greatest things. He is the one who gets the people to do the greatest things.

—*Ronald Reagan*

People ask the difference between a leader and a boss. The leader leads, and the boss drives.

—*Theodore Roosevelt*

Leadership is a potent combination of strategy and character. But if you must be without one, be without the strategy.

—*Norman Schwarzkopf*

Greatness consists of great men acting in great events . . . over the events we have no control, they either find us or they pass us by. All we can do is to ensure that they do not find us unprepared.

—*General William "Baldy" Smith*

Men make history and not the other way around. In periods where there is no leadership, society stands still. Progress occurs when courageous, skillful leaders seize the opportunity to change things for the better.

—*Harry S. Truman*

Leadership is the art of getting other people to run with your idea as if it were their own.

—*Harry S. Truman*

PEACE

A decade has passed since my service as president of the American Red Cross took me to Goma, Zaire—now Congo—but the memories of that trip are still very fresh in my mind. Rwanda had been devastated not by a natural disaster, but by a man made disaster: civil war. One million Rwandans had crossed the border into Zaire in hopes of escaping the horrifying mass killings the war had brought about. They stopped at the worst possible place—on volcanic rock. They couldn't dig for latrines, and cholera and dysentery were rampant. Digging individual graves was also impossible, and twice a day bodies were simply hauled off to a mass grave. As I made my way through the camp, I literally had to step over dead bodies.

To this day, I can close my eyes and see a boy sitting all by himself on a mound of African dirt. He was probably thirteen or fourteen— all arms and legs and feet, as most boys are at that age. His face was covered with dust, and he was crying. I sat beside him to try to comfort him, but there was no reaction. He was traumatized, and nothing moved, except the tears, which left little paths down both his cheeks.

Outside one of the tents, a semiconscious woman lay dying of cholera. At her side, a child cried piteously for milk and comfort its mother could no longer give. As I walked hand-in-hand through the camp, another child, about six years old, came up to me and took my hand. He walked with me wherever I went.

I wonder where he is now. What kind of future is there for him and for the thousands upon thousands of other children who were orphaned by the civil war? What we must work for is a future where all children can live in peace.

Peace cannot be kept by force, it can only be achieved by understanding.

—Albert Einstein

Peace signifies more than the stilling of guns, easing the sorrow of war. More than escape from death, it is a way of life. More than a haven for the weary, it is hope for the brave.

—Dwight David Eisenhower

I think that people want peace so much that one of these days governments had better get out of their way and let them have it.

—Dwight David Eisenhower

The pursuit of peace resembles the building of a great cathedral. It is the work of a generation. In concept, it requires a master architect. In execution, the labors of many.

—Hubert H. Humphrey

Let us not accept violence as the way to peace. Let us instead begin by respecting true freedom. The resulting peace will be able to satisfy the world's expectations, for it will be a peace built on justice, a peace founded on the incomparable dignity of the free human being.

—Pope John Paul II

Peace is a daily, a weekly, a monthly process, gradually changing opinions, slowly eroding old barriers, quietly building new structures. And however undramatic the pursuit of peace, the pursuit must go on.

—John F. Kennedy

I refuse to accept the view that mankind is so tragically bound to the starless midnight of racism and war that the bright daybreak of peace and brotherhood can never become a reality. I believe that unarmed truth and unconditional love will have the final word.

—Martin Luther King, Jr.

You cannot shake hands with a clenched fist.

—Golda Meir

Peace is like a delicate plant. It has to be constantly tended to and nurtured if it is to survive. If we neglect it, it will wither and die.

—Richard Nixon

The greatest honor history can bestow is the title
of peacemaker.

—*Richard Nixon*

Peace is the highest aspiration of the American people.
We will negotiate for it, sacrifice for it; we will not sur-
render for it, now or ever.

—*Ronald Reagan*

It isn't enough to talk about peace; one must believe in it.
And it isn't enough to believe in it; one must work at it.

—*Eleanor Roosevelt*

When the bells of peace ring, there will be no hands to
beat the drums of war. Even if they existed, they would
be stilled.

—*Anwar el-Sadat*

Peace is not the work of a single day, nor will it be the consequence of a single act. Yet every constructive act contributes to its growth; every omission impedes it. Peace will come, in the end, if it comes at all, as a child grows to maturity—slowly, imperceptibly, until we realize one day in incredulous surprise that the child is almost grown.

—Adlai Stevenson

Our goal must be not peace in our time, but peace for all time.

—Harry S. Truman

To be prepared for war is one of the most effectual means of preserving peace.

—George Washington

SOLDIERS AND VETERANS

When General George C. Marshall was asked during World War II if America had a secret weapon that would ensure victory, he replied, "America's secret weapon is the best darned kids in the world." Those words were true in the 1940s, when Bob Dole and so many others of his generation risked their lives for freedom, and in the sixty years that have followed, in places like Korea, Vietnam, Afghanistan and Iraq. One of the true privileges of representing North Carolina in the United States Senate is the opportunity to visit the many military facilities in our state and to meet and thank the men and women who wear our country's uniform. Freedom will always survive as long as America produces "the best darned kids in the world."

The long roll call, all the G.I. Joes and Janes, all the ones who fought faithfully for freedom, who hit the ground and sucked the dust and knew their share of horror: This may seem frivolous, and I don't mean it so, but it's moving to me how the world saw them. The world saw not only their special valor but their special style: their rambunctious, optimistic bravery; their do-or-die unity unhampered by class or race or region. What a group we've put forth, for generations now—from the ones who wrote "Kilroy was here" on the walls of the German stalags to those who left signs in the Iraqi desert that said, "I saw Elvis." What a group of kids we've sent out into the world.

—George H. W. Bush

The gratitude of every home in our Island, in our Empire, and indeed throughout the world, except in the abodes of the guilty, goes out to the British Airmen who, undaunted by odds, unwearied in their constant challenge and mortal danger, are turning the tide of the world war by their prowess and by their devotion. Never in the field of human conflict was so much owed by so many to so few.

—Winston Churchill

The nation which forgets its defenders will itself
be forgotten.

—*Calvin Coolidge*

On the one hand, war represents the ultimate failure of
mankind. Or at least the politicians and diplomats
entrusted with keeping the peace. Yet it also summons
the greatest qualities of which human beings are capable:
courage beyond measure, loyalty beyond words, sacrifice
and ingenuity and endurance beyond imagining.

—*Bob Dole*

Every good citizen makes his country's honor his own,
and cherishes it not only as precious, but as sacred. He is
willing to risk his life in its defense, and is conscious
that he gains protection while he gives it.

—*Andrew Jackson*

Since this country was founded, each generation of Americans has been summoned to give testimony to its national loyalty. The graves of young Americans who answered the call to service surround the globe.

—*John F. Kennedy*

This extraordinary war in which we are engaged falls heavily upon all classes of people, but most heavily upon the soldier. For it has been said, all that a man hath will he give for his life; and while all contribute of their substance the soldier puts his life at stake, and often yields it up in his country's cause. The highest merit, then, is due to the soldier.

—*Abraham Lincoln*

The soldier above all other people prays for peace, for he must suffer and bear the deepest wounds and scars of war.

—*Douglas MacArthur*

The soldier is the army. No army is better than its soldiers. The soldier is also a citizen. In fact, the highest obligation and privilege of citizenship is that of bearing arms for one's country. Hence it is a proud privilege to be a soldier—a good soldier. To be a soldier a man must have discipline, self-respect, pride in his unit and in his country, a high sense of duty and obligation to his comrades and to his superiors, and self-confidence born of demonstrated ability.

—*General George S. Patton, Jr.*

Over the years, the United States has sent many of its fine young men and women into great peril to fight for freedom beyond our borders. The only amount of land we have ever asked for in return is enough to bury those who did not return.

—*Colin Powell*

They weren't warriors. They were American boys who by mere chance of fate had wound up with guns in their hands, sneaking up a death-laden street in a strange and shattered city in a faraway country in a driving rain. They were afraid, but it was beyond their power to quit. They had no choice. They were good boys. I talked with them all afternoon as we sneaked slowly forward along the mysterious and rubbled streets, and I know they were good boys. And even though they weren't warriors born to kill, they won their battles. That's the point.

—*Ernie Pyle*

In James Michener's book, *The Bridges at Toko-Ri,* he writes of an officer waiting through the night for the return of planes to a carrier as dawn is coming on. And he asks, "Where do we find such men?" Well, we find them where we've always found them. They are the product of the freest society man has ever known. They make a commitment to the military—make it freely, because the birthright we share as Americans is worth defending.

—*Ronald Reagan*

The men of Normandy had faith that what they were doing was right, faith that they fought for all humanity, faith that a just God would grant them mercy on this beachhead or on the next. It was the deep knowledge— and pray God we have not lost it—that there is a profound, moral difference between the use of force for liberation and the use of force for conquest.

—*Ronald Reagan*

It doesn't take a hero to order men into battle. It takes a hero to be one of those men who go into battle.

—*General H. Norman Schwarzkopf*

WOMEN

Frances Perkins, who as Franklin Roosevelt's Secretary of Labor was the first female Cabinet officer in American history, was once asked if being a woman posed a disadvantage in public life. "Only," she said, "when I am climbing trees."

Of all the changes I have witnessed during my nearly four decades in public service, the change in the opportunities available to women and minorities is probably the greatest. I will never forget my first day at Harvard Law School. There were 550 members of the class of 1965—only two dozen of them women. A male student approached me and asked, "Elizabeth, what are you doing here? Don't you realize that there are men who would give their right arm to be in this law school, men who would use their legal education?" I guarantee you that question is not asked of the women who now comprise roughly 50 percent of each Harvard Law School class!

I also vividly recall a time in the late 1960s when I was serving in the White House Office of Consumer Affairs, and I was asked to attend a meeting at a downtown Washington, D.C. club. I arrived at the front door of the club and identified myself to the doorman as Elizabeth Hanford from the White House. The doorman replied, "I don't care if you're Queen Elizabeth. You can't go in, this club is for men only."

While much progress has been made in the past several decades, there is still more to do. Here are some words to keep in mind:

Do not put such unlimited power into the hands of the husbands. Remember all men would be tyrants if they could. If particular care is not paid to the ladies, we are determined to foment a rebellion, and will not hold ourselves bound by any laws in which we have no voice, no representation.

—*Abigail Adams*

The true republic: men, their rights and nothing more; women, their rights, and nothing less.

—*Susan B. Anthony*

Superiority we've always had; all we ask is equality.

—*Lady Nancy Astor*

Please know that I am aware of the hazards. I want to do it because I want to do it. Women must try to do things as men have tried. When they fail, their failure must be a challenge to others.

—*Amelia Earhart*

Toughness doesn't have to come in a pinstripe suit.

—*Dianne Feinstein*

There is in every woman's heart a spark of heavenly fire which lies dormant in the broad daylight of prosperity, but which kindles up and beams and blazes in the dark hour of adversity.

—*Washington Irving*

Women, if the soul of the nation is to be saved, I believe
that you must become its soul.

> —*Coretta Scott King*

A woman is like a tea bag. It's only when she's in hot
water that you realize how strong she is.

> —*Nancy Reagan*

There is a growing strength in women, but it is in the
forehead, not in the forearm.

> —*Beverly Sills*

In politics, if you want anything said, ask a man; if you
want anything done, ask a woman.

> —*Margaret Thatcher*

. . . If anyone asks me what I think the chief cause of the
extraordinary prosperity and growing power of [America], I
should answer that it is due to the superiority of their women.

> —*Alexis de Tocqueville*

WORK

Throughout my life, no one provided me with more good advice and more common sense than my mother, Mary Hanford. While Mother's family and friends could take solace in the fact that she lived a long and rewarding life, her death in early 2004 at the age of 102 still left us mourning the fact that we would not be able to have our daily chats and benefit from her wisdom and insights.

I especially recall a conversation with Mother soon after I accepted the job as president of the American Red Cross. Mother remembered that during World War II, she had been a Red Cross volunteer, and she said, "Nothing I ever did made me feel so important."

Often when I speak to an audience of high school or college students, I share that story, and I urge them to search for something they feel passionately about—to find a sense of mission, be it in the workplace, as a volunteer, or as a parent, that causes them to say "Nothing I ever did made me feel so important."

There are no menial jobs, only menial attitudes.

—William J. Bennett

The secret of joy in work is contained in one word—
excellence. To know how to do something well is to
enjoy it.

—Pearl Buck

Fall in love with what you are going to do for a living.
To be able to get out of bed and do what you love to do
for the rest of the day is beyond words. I'd rather be a
failure in something that I love than be successful in
something that I hate.

—George Burns

Are you bored with life? Then throw yourself into some
work you believe in with all your heart; live for it, die for
it, and you will find happiness that you had thought
could never be yours.

—Dale Carnegie

166

~ Work

To find out what one is fitted to do, and to secure an opportunity to do it, is the key to happiness.

—*John Dewey*

I never did a day's work in my life—it was all fun.

—*Thomas A. Edison*

The three great essentials to achieve anything worth-while are, first, hard work; second, stick-to-itiveness; third, common sense.

—*Thomas A. Edison*

Quality means doing it right when no one is looking.

—*Henry Ford*

To love what you do, and feel that it matters. How could anything else be more fun?

—*Katherine Graham*

No one should retire from work. If he does, he will shrivel up into a nuisance—talking to everybody about pains and pills and income tax. When I'm not working, I get tired of myself.

—*Herbert Hoover*

I'm a great believer in luck, and I find the harder I work, the more I have of it.

—*Thomas Jefferson*

I long to accomplish a great and noble task, but it is my chief duty to accomplish humble tasks as though they were great and noble. The world is moved along, not only by the mighty shove of heroes, but also by the tiny pushes of each honest worker.

—*Helen Keller*

No work is insignificant. All work that uplifts humanity has dignity and importance, and should be undertaken with painstaking excellence. If a man is called to be a streetsweeper, he should sweep streets even as Michelangelo painted, or Beethoven composed music, or Shakespeare wrote poetry. He should sweep streets so well that all the host of heaven and earth will pause to say, "Here lived a great streetsweeper who did his job well."

—Martin Luther King, Jr.

Real success is finding your life's work in the work that you love.

—David McCullough

Think enthusiastically about everything; but especially about your job. If you do so, you'll put a touch of glory in your life. If you love your job with enthusiasm, you'll shake it to pieces.

—Norman Vincent Peale

The road to happiness lies in two simple principles: find what interests you and that you can do well, and put your whole soul in it—every bit of energy and ambition and natural ability you have.

—*John D. Rockefeller III*

If you want to be successful, know what you are doing, love what you are doing, and believe in what you are doing.

—*Will Rogers*

Happiness lies not in the mere possession of money; it lies in the joy of achievement, in the thrill of the creative effort.

—*Franklin D. Roosevelt*

Far and away, the best prize life has to offer is the chance to work hard at work worth doing.

—*Theodore Roosevelt*

I feel that the greatest reward for doing is the opportunity to do more.

—Dr. Jonas Salk

Look at a day when you are supremely satisfied at the end. It's not a day when you lounge around doing nothing. It's when you've had everything to do, and you've done it.

—Margaret Thatcher

The secret of success is making your vocation a vacation.

—Mark Twain

The best preparation for work is not thinking about work, talking about work, or studying for work: It is work.

—William Weld

What I know is, is that if you do work that you love, and the work fulfills you, the rest will come.

—Oprah Winfrey

Success is peace of mind in knowing you did your best.

—John Wooden

YOUTH AND THE FUTURE

Shortly after graduating from Duke University, I spent part of a summer as a secretary in the office of North Carolina Senator B. Everett Jordan. While on Capitol Hill, I sought out Maine Senator Margaret Chase Smith, known as "the conscience of the Senate," and one of only two women in the Senate at that time. I don't know how many senators would share an hour with a twenty-two-year-old stranger seeking career advice, but that is just what she did. Senator Smith recommended that since my interests were government and public policy, I should continue my education by seeking a law degree.

In gratitude to Senator Smith, I try to meet with young women who ask to visit with me, answering their questions about public service careers, and offering advice on pitfalls that might await as they work their way up the ladder.

Destiny is not a matter of chance, it is a matter of choice; it is not a thing to be waited for, it is a thing to be achieved.

—*William Jennings Bryan*

The young do not know enough to be prudent, and therefore they attempt the impossible—and achieve it, generation after generation.

—*Pearl Buck*

If we were logical, the future would be bleak indeed. But we are more than logical. We are human beings, and we have faith, and we have hope, and we can work.

—*Jacques Cousteau*

Fortunately for us and our world, youth is not easily discouraged.

—*Dwight David Eisenhower*

It is while we are young that the habit of industry is formed. If not then, it never is afterwards. The fortune of our lives, therefore, depends on employing well the short period of youth.

—*Thomas Jefferson*

I like the dreams of the future better than the history of the past.

—*Thomas Jefferson*

Yesterday is not ours to recover, but tomorrow is ours to win or lose.

—*Lyndon Johnson*

The greatest natural resource that any country can have is its children.

—*Danny Kaye*

It is not possible for civilization to flow backward while there is youth in the world.

—*Helen Keller*

The best thing about the future is that it comes only one day at a time.

—*Abraham Lincoln*

The great contribution we can make is to prepare the oncoming generation to think that they can and will think for themselves.

—*Charles H. Mayo*

Challenge young people by having high expectations of them.

—*Colin Powell*

The house we hope to build is not for my generation but for yours. It is your future that matters. And I hope that when you are my age, you will be able to say as I have been able to say: We lived in freedom. We lived lives that were a statement, not an apology.

—Ronald Reagan

The future of our nation will be determined more than anything else by the character of our children.

—Ronald Reagan

We cannot always build the future for our youth, but we can build our youth for the future.

—Franklin D. Roosevelt

The future belongs to those who believe in the beauty of their dreams.

—*Eleanor Roosevelt*

The strongest and sweetest song remains to be sung.

—*Walt Whitman*

A FINAL THOUGHT

Perhaps my favorite historical anecdote is the story of the night in 1945 when General Dwight Eisenhower was walking along the banks of the Rhine River, thinking of the crossing in which he would lead the allied Armies. He met a soldier, and asked him why he wasn't sleeping. The young GI, who didn't recognize Ike, said, "I guess I'm just a little nervous."

"So am I," said Eisenhower. "Let's walk together, and perhaps we'll draw strength from one another."

It is my hope that you, the readers of this book, will find words from which you might draw strength. And now that I've shared my file with you, perhaps there are those out there who have a favorite inspiring quote or thought that was not included in this collection. If that's the case, please mail it to me c/o Carroll & Graf Publishers, 245 W. 17th St., New York, NY 10011. I would be honored to add it to my file, and—who knows—it just might find its way into a second volume of quotations so that more hearts can be touched with fire.

CONTRIBUTORS

Following is a list of those who provided the inspiring words found in this book. It seems insufficient to describe Winston Churchill as just a "British statesman" or Martin Luther King as an "American clergyman and civil rights leader," but space limitations required only very brief summaries. If there is a quote that you find especially inspiring, then I would encourage you to read more about the life of the man or woman behind those words.

Adams, Abigail; 1744–1818; Wife of John Adams, second
    president of the United States; mother of John Quincy
    Adams, sixth president of the United States

Adams, John; 1735–1826; Second president of the United
    States

Adams, John Quincy; 1767–1848; Sixth president of the
    United States

Alcott, Louisa May; 1832–1888; American author

Angelou, Maya; 1924–; American author, poet, playwright

Anthony, Susan B.; 1820–1906; American suffragist and social activist

Aquinas, St. Thomas; 1225–1274; Italian theologian and philosopher

Aquino, Corazon; 1933–; First woman president of the Philippines

Astor, Nancy; 1879–1964; First woman elected to serve in British Parliament

Baldwin, James; 1924–1987; American author

Barrie, James M.; 1860–1937; Scottish playwright and novelist

Barrymore, John; 1882–1942; American actor

Baruch, Bernard; 1870–1965; American statesman and financier

Beecher, Henry Ward; 1813–1887; American clergyman

Bell, Alexander Graham; 1847–1922; Scottish-born inventor

Bennett, William; 1944–; American educator, public official, author

Benson, Ezra Taft; 1899–1994; American public official and religious leader

Bergman, Ingrid; 1915–1982; Swedish-born actress

Bethune, Mary McLeod; 1875–1955; American civil-rights leader and humanitarian

Billings, Josh; 1818–1885; American humorist

Blair, Tony; 1953–; British politician and statesman

Bok, Derek; 1930–; American educator

Bombeck, Erma; 1927–1996; American columnist and author

Boorstin, Daniel; 1914–2004; American historian
    and author

Borge, Victor; 1909–2000; Danish-born pianist
    and humorist

Brandeis, Louis; 1856–1941; American jurist; justice of
    United States Supreme Court

Browning, Robert; 1812–1889; English poet and author

Bronte, Charlotte; 1816–1855; English poet and author

Bryan, William Jennings; 1860–1925; American politician
    and statesman

Buck, Pearl; 1892–1973; American author and novelist

Burke, Edmund; 1729–1797; British statesman

Burns, George; 1896–1996; American actor
    and humorist

Bush, Barbara; 1925–; American first lady; wife of George
    H. W. Bush

Bush, George Herbert Walker; 1924–; American politician;
    41st president of the United States

Bush, George W.; 1946–; American politician and statesman;
    43rd president of the United States

Byrnes, James F.; 1879–1972; American politican, jurist, and statesman

Carnegie, Dale; 1888–1955; American author

Carver, George Washington; 1865–1943; American educator and scientist

Cerf, Bennett; 1898–1971; American author and critic

Chesterton, G. K.; 1874–1936; English author and poet

Chisholm, Shirley; 1924–; American politician and civil-rights leader

Churchill, Winston; 1874–1965; British statesman

Coleridge, Samuel Taylor; 1772–1834; English poet

Conant, James Bryant; 1893–1978; American educator and scientist

Cooke, Alistair; 1908–2004; Author, broadcaster, and journalist

Coolidge, Calvin; 1872–1933; American politican and statesman; 30th president of the United States

Cooney, Joan Ganz; 1929–; American television producer

Cousteau, Jacques; 1910–1997; French-born oceanographer and author

cummings, e.e.; 1894–1962; American poet

Darrow, Clarence; 1857–1938; American attorney

Dewey, John; 1859–1952; American educator

Diana, Princess; 1961–1997; British princess;
    humanitarian

Dickens, Charles; 1812–1870; English author

Diefenbaker, John; 1895–1979; Canadian politician

Disraeli, Benjamin; 1804–1881; British statesman

Dole, Bob; 1923–; American politician and statesman

Earhart, Amelia; 1898–1937; American aviation pioneer

Edelman, Marian Wright; 1939–; American lawyer
    and social activist

Edison, Thomas; 1847–1931; American inventor

Einstein, Albert; 1879–1955; Scientist and physicist

Eisenhower, Dwight David; 1890–1969; American
    statesman and military leader; 34th president of the
    United States

Eliot, George; 1819–1890; English author

Ellington, Duke; 1899–1974; American jazz musician

Emerson, Ralph Waldo; 1803–1882; American poet and author

Evans, Richard L.; 1906–1971; American author and
    broadcaster

Fairless, Benjamin; 1890–1962; American business leader

Feinstein, Dianne; 1933–; American politician

Fitzgerald, F. Scott; 1896–1940; American author

Forbes, Malcolm; 1919–1990; American publisher and
    businessman

Ford, Gerald; 1913–; American statesman and politician;
  38th president of the United States

Ford, Henry; 1863–1947; American businessman

Frank, Anne; 1929–1945; German-born diarist and Holo-
  caust victim

Franklin, Benjamin; 1706–1790; American colonial leader,
  statesman, inventor, author

Friedman, Milton; 1912–; American economist

Frost, Robert; 1874–1963; American poet

Galbraith, John Kenneth; 1908–; Canadian-born economist

Gandhi, Mohandas K.; 1869–1948; Indian political and
  religious leader

Gardner, John; 1912–; American public official

Garfield, James A.; 1831–1881; American statesman and
  politician; 20th president of the United States

George, David Lloyd; 1863–1945; British statesman

Giamatti, A. Bartlett; 1938–1989; American educator
  and baseball administrator

Glenn, John; 1921–; American astronaut and politician

Goodwin, Doris Kearns; 1943–; American historian
  and author

Graham, Billy; 1918–; American evangelist

Graham, Katherine; 1917–2001; American businesswoman
  and publisher

Green, Theodore; 1867–1966; American politician

Gretzky, Wayne; 1961–; Canadian-born professional athlete

Gunther, John; 1901–1970; American author and journalist

Haley, Alex; 1921–1992; American author

Hammarskjold, Dag; 1905–1961; Swedish diplomat

Hand, Learned; 1872–1961; American jurist

Harvey, Paul; 1919–; American broadcaster and commentator

Hayes, Helen; 1900–1993; American actress

Hesburgh, Theodore; 1917–; American educator and author

Holmes, Oliver Wendell, Jr.; 1841–1935; American jurist

Holmes, Oliver Wendell, Sr.; 1809–1894; American author and physician

Hoover, Herbert; 1874–1964; American statesman and business leader; 31st president of the United States

Hope, Bob; 1903–2003; American actor, comedian, and humanitarian

Hugo, Victor; 1802–1885; French author and playwright

Humphrey, Hubert; 1911–1978; American politician and statesman

Iacocca, Lee; 1924–; American business executive

Ickes, Harold; 1874–1952; American lawyer and politician

Ingersoll, Robert G.; 1833–1899; American lawyer and lecturer

Irving, Washington; 1783–1859; American author

Jackson, Andrew; 1767–1845; American military leader and statesman; 7th president of the United States

James, William; 1842–1910; Philosopher

Jefferson, Thomas; 1743–1826; American statesman; 3rd president of the United States

Pope John Paul II; 1920–; Polish religious leader

Johnson, Claudia Alta "Lady Bird"; 1912–; Wife of Lyndon Johnson, 36th president of the United States

Johnson, Lyndon; 1908–1973; American politican; 36th president of the United States

Kaye, Danny; 1913–1987; American entertainer

Keller, Helen; 1880–1968; American author, lecturer, and humanitarian

Kennedy, Edward M.; 1932–; American politician

Kennedy, John F.; 1917–1963; American politician; 35th president of the United States

Kennedy, Robert F.; 1925–1968; American politician

King, Coretta Scott; 1929–; American civil-rights activist; wife of Martin Luther King, Jr.

King, Larry; 1933–; American broadcaster

King, Martin Luther; 1929–1968; American clergyman and civil-rights leader

Kissinger, Henry; 1923–; American public official and diplomat

Koop, C. Everett; 1916–; American physician and public health leader

Koppel, Ted; 1940–; American broadcast journalist

Krzyzewski, Mike; 1947–; American basketball coach

L'Amour, Louis; 1908–1988; American author

Lee, Robert E.; 1807–1872; American military leader

Lewis, C. S.; 1889–1963; British author

Lincoln, Abraham; 1809–1865; American statesman; 16th president of the United States

Lindbergh, Anne Morrow; 1906–2001; American poet and essayist; wife of American aviator Charles Lindbergh

Lippman, Walter; 1888–1974; American author and journalist

Long, Russell; 1918–2003; American politician

Loren, Sophia; 1934–; Italian actress

Luce, Clare Boothe; 1903–1987; American politician, writer, and diplomat

Luce, Henry; 1898–1967; American businessman and publisher

MacArthur, Douglas; 1880–1964; American military leader

MacLeish, Archibald; 1892–1982; Poet

Mandela, Nelson; 1918–; South African statesman and civil-rights leader

Mann, Horace; 1796–1859; American educator

Marshall, Thurgood; 1908–1993; American jurist

Marx, Groucho; 1890–1977; American comedian and actor

Mayo, Charles H.; 1865–1939; American physician and philanthropist; Co-founder of Mayo Clinic

McAuliffe, Christa; 1948–1986; American teacher and astronaut

McCain, John; 1936–; American politician

McCall, Tom; 1913–1983; American politician

McCullough, David; 1933–; American historian and author

Mead, Margaret; 1901–1978; American anthropologist and author

Meir, Golda; 1898–1978; Israeli political leader

Michener, James; 1907–1997; American author

Monroe, James; 1758–1831; American statesman; 5th president of the United States

Montgomery, Bernard; 1887–1976; British military leader

Moses, Anna Mary "Grandma"; 1860–1961; American painter

Murrow, Edward; 1908–1965; American journalist and broadcaster

Nixon, Richard M.; 1913–1994; American politician; 37th president of the United States

O'Neill, Thomas P. "Tip"; 1912–1994; American politician

Paige, Leroy "Satchel"; 1906–1982; American baseball player

Paine, Thomas; 1737–1809; American patriot and author

Parks, Rosa; 1913–; American civil-rights leader

Parton, Dolly; 1946–; American singer, actress, entertainer

Patton, George S., Jr.; 1885–1945; American military leader

Pasteur, Louis; 1822–1895; French chemist and scientist

Pearl, Minnie; 1912–1996; American entertainer

Peale, Norman Vincent; 1898–1993; American clergyman and author

Penn, William; 1644–1718; English religious leader; founder of Pennsylvania

Peterson, Esther; 1906–1996; American labor, women's rights, and consumer activist

Powell, Colin; 1937–; American diplomat, military leader

Price, Joseph Charles; 1854–1893; American educator

Pyle, Ernie; 1900–1945; American journalist

Rankin, Jeanette; 1880–1973; American politician and social activist

Rather, Dan; 1931–; American journalist and author

Rayburn, Sam; 1882–1961; American politician

Reagan, Nancy; 1923–; American First Lady; wife of Ronald Reagan

Reagan, Ronald; 1911–2004; American politician; 40th president of the United States

Rickover, Hyman; 1900–1986; American admiral

Robinson, Jackie; 1919–1972; American baseball player

Rockefeller, David; 1915–; American businessman and philanthropist

Rockefeller, John D., Sr.; 1839–1937; American businessman and philanthropist

Rockefeller, Nelson; 1908–1979; American politician

Rockne, Knute; 1888–1931; American football player and coach

Rogers, Fred; 1928–2003; American entertainer and educator

Rogers, Will; 1879–1935; American humorist

Rooney, Andy; 1919–; American author and commentator

Roosevelt, Eleanor; 1884–1962; American First Lady; wife of Franklin D. Roosevelt; writer, lecturer, and social activist

Roosevelt, Franklin D.; 1882–1945; American politician and statesman; 32nd president of the United States

Roosevelt, Theodore; 1858–1919; American politician and statesman; 26th president of the United States

Rubinstein, Arthur; 1887–1982; Polish-born pianist

el-Sadat, Anwar; 1918–1981; Egyptian military leader and politician

Safire, William; 1929–; American journalist and novelist

Salk, Jonas; 1914–1995; American medical scientist

Sandburg, Carl; 1878–1967; American poet and author

Schlossberg, Caroline Kennedy; 1957–; American author; daughter of John F. Kennedy

Schwarzkopf, H. Norman; 1934–; American military leader

Schultz, Charles; 1922–2000; American cartoonist

Schurz, Carl; 1829–1906; American public official

Schweitzer, Albert; 1875–1965; French theologian and humanitarian

Shaw, George Bernard; 1856–1950; Irish playwright

Shriver, Sargent; 1915–; American public servant and diplomat

Sills, Beverly; 1929–; American opera singer

Simon, Neil; 1927–; American playwright

Simpson, Alan; 1936–; American politician

Skinner, B. F.; 1904–1990; American psychologist

Smith, Alfred E.; 1873–1944; American politician

Smith, Margaret Chase; 1897–1995; American politician

Smith, William "Baldy"; 1824–1903; American military leader

Stevenson, Adlai; 1900–1965; American politician and diplomat

Stevenson, Robert Louis; 1850–1894; Scottish author and poet

Stowe, Harriet Beecher; 1811–1896; American author

Tarbell, Ida; 1857–1944; American journalist

Mother Teresa; 1910–1997; Macedonia-born religious leader; humanitarian

Thackeray, William Makepeace; 1811–1863; English author

Thatcher, Margaret; 1925–; British politician; first woman prime minister of Great Britain

Thomas, Danny; 1914–1991; American entertainer

Thoreau, Henry David; 1817–1862; American writer

de Tocqueville, Alexis; 1805–1859; French social philosopher

Truman, Harry S.; 1884–1972; American politician; 33rd president of the United States

Tutu, Desmond; 1931–; South African religious and civil-rights leader

Twain, Mark; 1835–1910; American author and humorist

Van Buren, Abigail; 1918–; American newspaper columnist

Walesa, Lech; 1943–; Polish statesman

Walker, Mort; 1923–; American cartoonist

Warren, Earl; 1891–1974; American jurist and politician

Washington, Booker T.; 1856–1915; American educator

Washington, George; 1732–1799; American statesman; first president of the United States

Wayne, John; 1907–1979; American actor

Webster, Daniel; 1782–1852; American statesman

Weld, William; 1945–; American politician and author

Wells, H. G.; 1866–1946; English author

Wesley, John; 1703–1791; English clergyman

Wharton, Edith; 1862–1937; English author

Whitman, Walt; 1819–1892; American poet

Will, George; 1941–; American journalist

Wilson, Woodrow; 1856–1924; American statesman and politician; 28th president of the United States

Winfrey, Oprah; 1953–; American broadcaster and actress

Winters, Jonathan; 1925–; American comedian and entertainer

Wolfe, Thomas; 1900–1938; American author

Wooden, John; 1910–; American basketball coach and educator

Wright, Frank Lloyd; 1867–1959; American architect

Yeager, Chuck; 1923–; American pilot

Yeats, William Butler; 1865–1939; Irish poet and playwright